# Dresden Quilt Workshop

## Tips, Tools & Techniques for Perfect Mini Dresden Plates

Susan R. Marth

C&T PUBLISHING

Text copyright © 2017 by Susan R. Marth

Photography and artwork copyright © 2017 by C&T Publishing, Inc.

Publisher: Amy Marson

Creative Director: Gailen Runge

Editor: Monica Gyulai

Technical Editor: Del Walker

Cover/Book Designer: April Mostek

Production Coordinator: Tim Manibusan

Production Editors: Jeanie German and Alice Mace Nakanishi

Illustrator: Kirstie L. Pettersen

Photo Assistant: Mai Yong Vang

Style photography by Lucy Glover and instructional photography by Diane Pedersen of C&T Publishing, Inc., unless otherwise noted

Published by C&T Publishing, Inc., P.O. Box 1456, Lafayette, CA 94549

Library of Congress Cataloging-in-Publication Data

Names: Marth, Susan R., 1964- author.

Title: Dresden quilt workshop : tips, tools & techniques for perfect mini Dresden plates / Susan R. Marth.

Description: Lafayette, CA : C&T Publishing, Inc., [2017]

Identifiers: LCCN 2016058062 | ISBN 9781617455001 (soft cover)

Subjects: LCSH: Dresden plate quilts. | Quilting--Patterns. | Patchwork quilts.

Classification: LCC TT835 .M27295 2017 | DDC 746.46--dc23

LC record available at https://lccn.loc.gov/2016058062

Printed in the USA

10 9 8 7 6 5 4 3 2 1

# Dedication

*This book is dedicated to my amazing family. First, to my husband, David, for working so hard to give us a comfortable life so that I could have the best job in the world: being a stay-at-home mom for Chloe, Blake, and Clare (which led me to this quilting life). Second, to our children, who have always been so easy to love. I am so proud of you all.*

# Acknowledgments

**Thank you to my husband, David, and our children, Chloe, Blake, and Clare** for putting up with quilts in all their stages all over our house. Also, thanks for your help and encouragement.

**Thank you to my mom** for giving me your love of fabric and for teaching me to sew.

**Thank you to my dad** for teaching me to work hard and then to work some more.

**Thank you to C&T Publishing** for helping me put my love of little Dresden plates into this beautiful book.

**Thank you to Moda Fabrics** for generously providing me with beautiful fabric for the quilts in this book and for many other pattern samples through the years.

**Thank you to *all* my pattern editors, testers and quilt market helpers**—especially Robin Koehler, Kathy Sands, and Cindy Stutz.

**I'D ALSO LIKE TO THANK:**

**Tamara Lynn**, my machine quilter, for helping to make my quilts look wonderful.

**The Warm Company**, for the Warm and Natural cotton batting that I insist on using in all my quilt-as-you-go quilts.

**Sulky of America**, for wonderful cotton thread that enhances my designs, especially the appliqué.

**Quilt shops around the world**, for helping to sell my patterns.

**And especially to all the quilters who purchase and sew my patterns**, thanks!

# Contents

----------------------------------

# PROJECTS

Cross Roads   40

Star-Spangled Dresdens   45

Quilt-as-You-Go Button Box   51

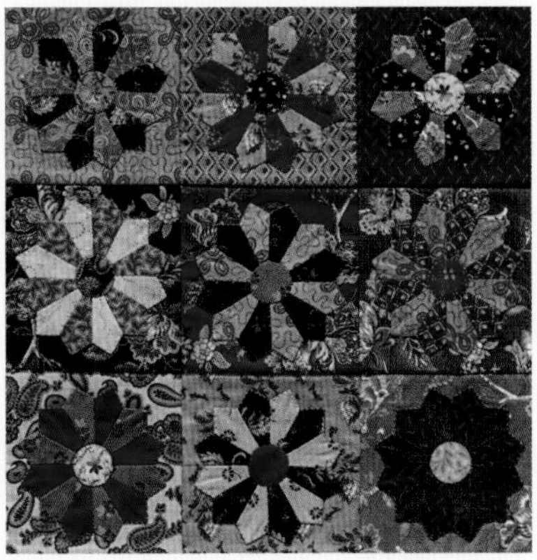

Shimmering Dresdens   57

Dresden Ohio   61

Follow Me   65

Spring Fair   70

Friendship Garden   75

All Roads Lead to Dresden   80

# Introduction

My mom taught me to sew as a child, first by hand with her scraps, then on her sewing machine making clothes for 4-H projects. The first project might sound familiar to some of you: a straight, gathered skirt and a triangle scarf. I was nine years old when I made my ensemble and chose fabric that showcased my childhood star, Raggedy Ann.

My sister Lori and I shared a bedroom with our mom's sewing corner. On many a night, we were lulled to sleep by the whir of her machine. Her days were spent tending to us kids (I'm number five of six) and doing farm chores. But she also sewed a lot of clothes for our family—sometimes staying up all night to finish our holiday dresses. As a child I thought that was crazy, but now I realize it was precious time carved away for creativity.

Ready for the runway, complete with coordinating purse

I went on to earn a bachelor's degree in interior architectural design, and started quilting after I became a stay-at-home mom by watching quilting programs on PBS. One of those shows, *Quilting from the Heartland*, required an apple core plastic template. In my search to get that specialty tool, I discovered local quilt shops—along with the end of life as I knew it!

The "applecore" quilt that started it all

Early on, I made a quilt top that was full of half-square triangles, and my mother-in-law arranged to have it quilted for me. I was congratulated by one of the quilters for doing a nice job for my "first try." I was a bit offended! Years later I could see that many of the points of my half-square triangles were less than perfect. I had no idea, back then, that points could be accurate or that there were tips and tricks for making them so.

Eventually I joined a local quilt guild, started altering patterns, and developed my own designs. In 2003, I started Suzn Quilts and began selling patterns to local quilt shops. Now in my twenty-fifth year, quilting has become more of a marathon than the sprint of my younger days. I still love to quilt every day and my "to-make" list of quilts keeps growing. I've developed techniques to achieve precision, and am excited to share them with you here.

While making the quilts for this book, I took the time to investigate every little step in detail so that I could convey each of those steps to you. I have developed little tricks and found just the right tools to make little Dresdens. No matter how many of these little gems I sew, my brain keeps dreaming up new designs.

These little blocks will steal your heart and they can be addictive. Indeed, Dresden plate quilts have been around for a very long time but these projects are not your grandma's Dresdens.

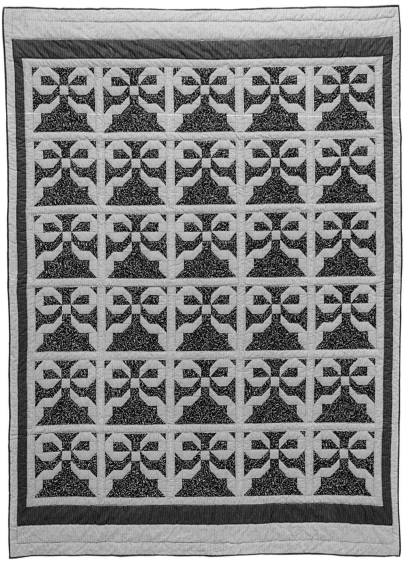

My points weren't perfect at first!

# Perfect Tools for Perfect Little Petals

Here's a list of supplies that make it easier to produce precise little Dresden plates. I've been using some of these tools for years, while others are recent discoveries. In addition to the listed products, I also recommend a sewing machine with a blind hem stitch that can be tweaked in terms of stitch length and width. If you can shorten the length and narrow the width, you can easily sew a practically invisible, tiny stitch that resembles hand sewing.

## A. Mary Ellen's Best Press

When working with small fabric pieces in particular it's very important, if not imperative, to add stability to the fabric. This is true even for top-quality quilt shop fabrics. Mary Ellen's Best Press adds body to fabric without making it stiff. I recommend having it in both the hand and single-finger pump bottles. For detailed usage instructions, refer to Best Press Dos and Don'ts (page 12).

## B. Suzn Quilts' Templates

Suzn Quilts' Tiny Dresden Plate Template #216 and Mini Dresden Plate Template #186 are optional. You can make your own templates from the paper patterns included in this book. However, I have manufactured plastic templates to make cutting the Tiny and Mini Dresden petals more accurate and much faster. Cut up to 8 layers of cotton fabric at once with a rotary cutter and these templates.

## C. Collins Fabric Grips

Stick Collins Fabric Grips to the back of plastic templates to keep them from slipping when cutting. They are especially helpful when cutting small pieces such as Dresden petals.

## D. Sulky 30-Weight Cotton Thread

Sulky 30-weight cotton in color #733-1180 is my favorite thread for sewing and appliquéing Dresden plates. This neutral taupe color blends with most every color of fabric I use and is a great choice when there are multiple petal colors in one plate. Surprisingly, it blends well with both lighter and darker colors. If I'm sewing plates with just a single fabric, I may select a thread that's a perfect match, though I often just stick with the taupe since it blends so well.

## E. Perfect Piecing Seam Guide by Perkins Dry Goods

Use the Perfect Piecing Seam Guide to find a perfect, scant ¼″ seam on your machine. It's imperative that your seams are accurate when sewing Dresden plates or they won't lie flat. For detailed instructions, refer to Setting up Your Machine with a Perfect Piecing Seam Guide (page 12).

## F. Open Embroidery Foot

I do just about all my sewing with an open embroidery foot (#20 BERNINA). The wide open pathway that extends to the needle makes it easy to be very accurate when appliquéing and piecing. I can achieve an accurate scant ¼″ seam allowance with this foot by moving my needle position one click to the right and aligning the edge of the foot with the fabric. The only time I change presser feet is to use a walking foot for straight quilting or binding, or to use a free-motion foot.

## G. Tiny Thread Cutting Scissors

To make Dresden plates that are free of thread tails, trim *really* close to the seams with tiny thread cutting scissors.

## H. Clover Bordeaux 5⅛″ Ultimate Scissors

Clover Bordeaux 5⅛″ Ultimate Scissors are extremely sharp and actually grip fabric while cutting. The grip makes it possible to cut very small pieces of fabric and to trim really close to seams. With these, you can cut out the bulk of a seam allowance to within threads of the seam, allowing for precise points on Dresden petals. The scissors come with a leather sheath to help protect your investment.

## I. That Purple Thang

That Purple Thang makes turning small points right side out a snap! Nothing is worse than poking a hole through the end of a petal then having to re-cut and sew another one. You will not have that issue with this tool owing to its rounded (yet pointed) small tip. The flat end also makes a nice pressing tool.

## J. Roxanne Glue-Baste-It

Roxanne Glue-Baste-It is the perfect glue for little Dresden pieces. A fine needle allows for controlled, hairline applications. The glue dries quickly so you can fold fabric around Dresden center templates without waiting. It also holds pieces firmly in place until they are sewn. When dampened for template removal it leaves no residue behind. I especially like the newer accordion shape bottle that pulls the glue from the needle applicator back down into the bottle so it does not dry up and clog the tip.

## K. Bohin Glue Stick

Bohin glue sticks are very handy, especially for touch-ups. I keep one at my sewing machine in case something is loose when I'm ready to appliqué it down. It's mess free and has a small tip for getting into small places.

## L. Freezer Paper

Freezer paper is easy to find in stores, inexpensive, transparent, and works great when making templates. Trace designs, cut them out, and press them with a dry iron to temporarily adhere them to the wrong side of fabric. Remove the paper without leaving a residue by just peeling it away.

## M. APLIQUICK Tools

APLIQUICK bars look a little like dental tools and enable you to maneuver small sections of fabric, such as the seam allowance of a Dresden plate circle. Apply glue around the circle on the seam allowance and then use these tools to fold back the fabric and stick it to the wrong side of the template. The glue will start to dry as you press the fabric to the wrong side of the paper template, but you will still be able to work out any little imperfections with these handy tools before the glue is totally set.

## N. Circle Paper Cutters

Circle paper punches make it easy to quickly and accurately cut six layers of freezer paper into perfect 1″ and 2″ circles. Many companies make circle cutters, though I prefer the EK Success brand. If you have any trouble using cutters, it's probably because you're not putting enough layers of paper in at once; I recommend six layers.

## O. Thangles

Use Thangles to make half-square triangles, saving time and fabric. It is much faster and accurate to cut fabric into strips and sew on paper rather than making individual half-square triangles. The company's instructions and hints are wonderful. I starch my fabric first and get perfect results every time. All projects in the book include cutting variations for using Thangles.

## P. Square Rulers

Use a ruler that's close in size to the fabric piece you are rotary cutting. I use a 6″ × 6″ square ruler to cut the Tiny Dresden 5″ × 5″ background squares and a 9½″ × 9½″ square ruler which is the size of the Mini Dresden background squares.

## Q. Rotating Mat

Cut petals from small fabric strips easily on a small rotating cutting mat. There is no need to shift the strips or walk around the cutting mat. Instead, trim the end of the strip and twist the board to start cutting petals. I use Fiskars 8″ × 8″ version.

## R. Omnigrid Mini Fold-Away

This all-in-one, 7″ × 7″ portable cutting mat and ironing surface is great for making little blocks anyplace that space is limited—in front of the TV or in a quilting class. Cut petals on the small mat and press them on the ironing surface right at your worktable using either a full-size or mini iron.

## S. Warm and Natural Cotton Batting

I only recommend Warm and Natural cotton batting for my quilt-as-you-go technique. It doesn't stretch in any direction and has properties that help keep the foundation layers stuck together, making it easier to work wrinkle free.

# Mini Classroom

## Best Press Dos and Don'ts

Spray Best Press on fabrics before doing any cutting and they will glide through the sewing machine. This is especially beneficial for the small pieces as they will not be pushed down into the throat plate by the needle with every stitch. This will also make the bias edges of the Dresden petals more stable.

I use Best Press in a hand pump bottle on yardage before cutting any strips for petals and the rest of the quilt, but as you read through the instructions on these pages you'll see that I also use more Best Press as I assemble both the Tiny and Mini Dresden plates. In the case of spraying during the assembly process, I use the single-finger pump bottle because it allows a very fine spray that will evenly coat *but not saturate* small fabric pieces. I use a hand pump bottle to spray larger pieces of fabric because it's quicker and there's no worry of over saturation in this instance.

## Setting Up Your Machine with a Perfect Piecing Seam Guide

In most instances of quilting, including making little Dresden plates, finding and sewing a *scant* ¼″ seam is imperative. Some sewing machines, like my BERNINA, make this task very easy, but others are a bit trickier. The Perfect Piecing Seam Guide by Perkins Dry Goods takes the guesswork out of finding an *exact* scant ¼″.

**1.** Place the guide under the raised presser foot then lower the needle of the sewing machine through the hole in the guide.

**2.** Set the presser foot on the guide so that the guide is parallel with the seam allowance lines on the throat plate. If you have a BERNINA like I do, moving the needle position one click to the right of center will put the edge of the guide perfectly in line with the edge of the #20 (open embroidery) foot. I can feed the fabric through the machine with it aligned to the right edge of the foot and get an exact scant ¼″ seam allowance.

**3.** If you cannot easily follow the edge of your presser foot, whether the scant ¼″ seam is under or outside the foot, then you'll need to mark your machine with a sticky note, masking tape or another method so you have something to follow.

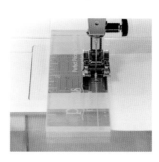

**4.** Once you have this guide marked, remove the seam guide and feed the fabric through your machine aligning it with the sticky note or whatever other option you've chosen to mark your machine with.

**5.** Practice the accuracy of your guide by cutting 2 squares of fabric 2″ × 2″ and sewing them together along 1 side. If your seam allowance is accurate, when you press the seam, the piece will measure 2″ × 3½″.

### Tip

If you have to mark your machine with a guide, keep the Perfect Piecing Seam Guide handy so when the guide needs replacing it's easy to find.

# Foolproof Binding

I enjoy binding quilts because I've figured out an easy way to sew the binding strips together and perfected a foolproof way of joining the two ends. No fancy tools are required and you can't tell where I joined the two ends because there's no bulky lump. Both of these techniques will work for straight of grain and bias binding. I always cut 2½″ binding strips unless the quilt warrants another size.

## Determine Quantity of Binding Strips

**1.** Add the length of the quilt to the width of the quilt and multiply this number by 2 to get the total length of binding needed (for example: 40″ + 60″ = 100″ × 2 = 200″).

**2.** Divide this number by 40 (the approximate width of the fabric, but if your fabric is narrower than 40″ use that number; 200/40 = 5). You will need 5 strips. If this number is not a whole number, you will need to round up (for example: 2½ strips is rounded up to 3 strips).

**3.** Cut 5 strips 2½″ × width of fabric. If making bias binding, the strips will be different lengths so you'll need to measure the strips until you reach the total length required.

## Sew Together the Binding Strips

**1.** Place the first binding strip on the cutting mat right side up with the top right corner of the strip aligned on a grid intersection. Place the second binding strip perpendicular to the first binding strip, with the top right corner aligned on the same grid square, but the opposite corner. The strips should be right sides together and the ends should overlap 1″ in both directions.

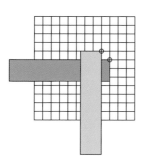

**2.** Place a 6″ ruler on top of the 2 strips with the ¼″ line of the ruler aligned to the ditch of the intersecting strips.

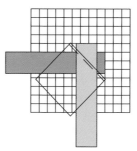

**3.** With a rotary cutter, cut off the ends of the strips.

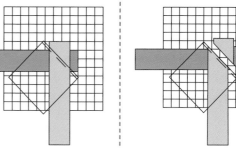

**4.** Pin together the 2 strips.

**5.** Repeat Steps 1–4 with the remaining 3 binding strips until all 5 strips are pinned together into one long strip.

**6.** Place 1 end of the strip *right side down* on the mat and trim the end at a 45° angle. This will be the start end of the strip.

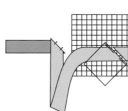

**7.** Stitch the pinned strips together with a scant ¼″ seam.

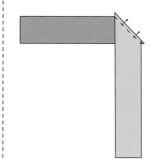

**8.** Press under ¼″ on the 45° start end of the strip, and then press the entire strip in half, with wrong sides together. Press the seams to 1 side.

## Stitch the Binding onto the Quilt

*For quilts that do not have blocks with points that come to the edge of the quilt, I trim the batting and backing to the edge of the quilt top and use ⅜" seam allowance to stitch the binding on. In instances where I have blocks with points that come to the edge of the quilt, I trim the batting and backing ⅛" larger than the top on all sides and still use ⅜" seam.*

**1.** Attach the walking foot and set the machine to stitch 7 stitches per inch. Place the binding on the quilt and check that the seams don't land at a corner. If any do, shift the binding.

**Tip: Start in the Middle**

**Place the starting end of the binding strip in the center of the bottom of the quilt. It keeps that seam away from any corners and it's easiest to join strips in the middle of a quilt edge.**

**2.** Leave a 6″ tail at the start end and sew on the binding, aligning the edge of the binding with the edge of the quilt.

**3.** Stop sewing ¼" from a corner, take a few backstitches, and remove the quilt from the machine.

**4.** Fold up the binding strip at a diagonal as shown.

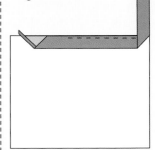

**5.** Fold down the binding strip so that the fold is even with the edge of the quilt. Start stitching at the edge of the quilt and continue to the next corner.

**6.** Repeat Steps 3–5 until all 4 corners are completed. Remove the quilt from the machine when you are within 6″ of the start end of the strip.

**7.** Trim the binding finish end 1″ past the start end as shown.

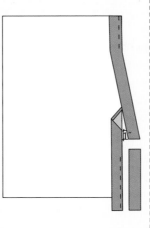

**8.** Place a pin in the finish end where it meets the ear of the fold.

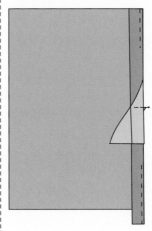

**9.** Align the unfolded ends of the binding strip at a 45° angle and pin in place. Stitch on the crease of the 45° start end.

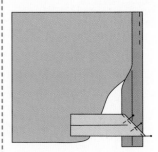

Aligning the crease of the start end with the edge of the finish end results in an overhang that creates a little ear.

**Tip: Remember!**

**Shorten your stitch length to piece the strips and then lengthen it again to finish applying the binding.**

**10.** Before trimming, refold the binding to make sure it fits and sits flat. If it doesn't, take out the stitches and redo.

**11.** Finish sewing the binding to the quilt.

**12.** Add a label as instructed in Label Your Quilts Painlessly (below).

**13.** Press the binding flat, as it was sewn, and then open it out and press again.

**14.** Use clips to hold the binding to the wrong side of the quilt and slip stitch it in place with thread that matches the binding fabric, mitering the corners.

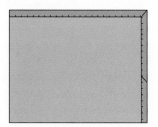

# Label Your Quilts Painlessly

Many of us fail to label our quilts. Maybe it feels like too much trouble near the end of a project because we're in a hurry to give the quilt away or just to be done. That's exactly the reason I use this technique to label all my quilts. A local quilt shop owner, Rosemary, showed me this method years ago and I have adopted it ever since.

**1.** Cut a strip of muslin 1½″ × 12″.

**Tip**

**Cut several strips 1½″ × width of fabric; subcut them into 12″ lengths and keep them next to your sewing machine so they're handy every time you finish a quilt. You'll label every quilt from now on!**

**2.** Press under ¼″ on both short ends.

**3.** Press the strip in half lengthwise.

**4.** Stitch the strip to the back of the quilt with ¼″ seam after the binding has been stitched to the front of the quilt but before it has been slip stitched to the back.

**5.** When you slip stitch the binding to the back of the quilt, stitch through the label too.

**6.** With a permanent pen, write pertinent information on the label. You can write on the back side of the strip too, or alter the length of the strip you cut if you have a lot to write on your label.

# Tiny and Mini Dresden Plate Assembly Techniques

**Finished Tiny Dresden Plate:**
approx. 3¾″ diameter
**Finished block:** 4½″ × 4½″

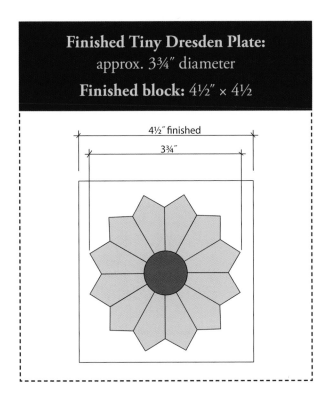

4½″ finished
3¾″

**Finished Mini Dresden Plate:**
approx. 7″ diameter
**Finished block:** 9″ × 9″

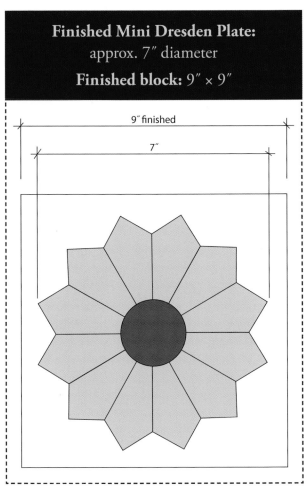

9″ finished
7″

It's no secret that I love to make little Dresden plates. I didn't realize *why* I enjoyed making them so much until I started teaching workshops to skilled quilters who didn't all share my appreciation for the process. It was then that I came to realize why my Dresdens go together easily and look seemingly perfect. Up until that point I thought I loved them because they're so darn cute! As it turns out, with the right tools and techniques, these plates go together effortlessly and lie perfectly flat every time. It's no wonder I love making them and you will too. So, collect your tools, follow along, and let's start making perfect little Dresdens.

**Tip: Dresden Plate Tips**

- Use high-quality cotton fabrics.

- Press each and every fabric with Mary Ellen's Best Press *before* doing any cutting.

- Press every seam flat, as sewn, to set the seam and then press as indicated.

- Sew scant ¼″ seam allowances or the plates will not lie flat. Consider using "Perfect Piecing Seam Guide" by Perkins Dry Goods to find the perfect seam allowance.

- Use more Best Press when indicated!

## Materials

*For descriptions of all specialty tools, refer to Perfect Tools for Perfect Little Petals (page 9).*

**Mary Ellen's Best Press:** In single-finger pump bottle

**Paper cutters:** 1″ and 2″ circles (recommended)

**Thread:** To match fabrics

**That Purple Thang**

**Fabric glue:** Such as Roxanne Glue-Baste-It

**Freezer paper**

### TINY DRESDEN PLATE

*For 1 block, you will need:*

**Petal fabric:** ¼ yard

**Center fabric:** Scrap

**Background fabric:** ¼ yard

### MINI DRESDEN PLATE

*For 1 block, you will need:*

**Petal fabric:** ¼ yard

**Center fabric:** Scrap

**Background fabric:** ⅓ yard

## Prepare the Fabrics

*Lightly spray each fabric with Mary Ellen's Best Press and then iron dry. For guidance, refer to Best Press Dos and Don'ts (page 12).*

## Cutting

### Tiny Dresden Plate

*For each block:*

#### Petal fabric

*To cut petal shapes, use the Tiny Dresden petal pattern (page 86) or Suzn Quilts' Tiny Dresden Template #216.*

• Cut 1 strip 2″ × 16″. Subcut into 12 petals as shown.

#### Center fabric

• Cut 1 square 1½″ × 1½″.

#### Background fabric

• Cut 1 square 5″ × 5″.

### Mini Dresden Plate

*For each block:*

#### Petal fabric

*To cut petal shapes, use the Mini Dresden petal pattern (page 86) or Suzn Quilts' Mini Dresden Template #186.*

• Cut 1 strip 3½″ × 23″. Subcut into 12 petals as shown.

#### Center fabric

• Cut 1 square 2½″ × 2½″.

#### Background fabric

• Cut 1 square 9½″ × 9½″.

# Assemble Dresden Plate Blocks

## Petals

**1.** Fold each petal in half with right sides together. Sew the wider end toward the fold with a scant ¼" seam, *using short stitches*.

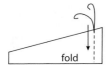

### Tip: Chainstitch Your Petals

You will save time and thread by sewing a petal seam, lifting the presser foot, and starting the seam for the next petal without cutting any thread. The 12 petals will be attached in 1 strip when you remove them from the machine. It's fast and you won't need to search for stray petals when it's time to trim them in the next step.

**2.** With small, sharp scissors, trim the seam allowance away from the fold, as shown.

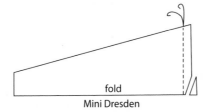

**3.** Press the seam to set.

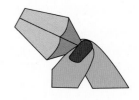

**4.** Press the entire folded petal to crease it for aligning purposes later.

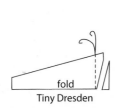

**5.** While holding the seam allowance to one side, turn the petal right side out.

**6.** Once turned, align the seam with the creased fold line.

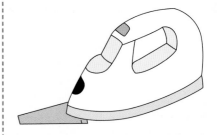

**7.** Using That Purple Thang or another blunt point, gently poke out the point of the petal while keeping the seam and the fold aligned.

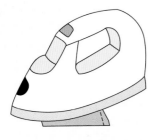

**8.** Keeping the seam and the fold line aligned, finger press the seam between your thumbnail and index finger a couple of times until the tip of the point is flat. This will set the seam.

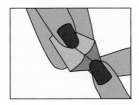

**9.** Keeping the seam aligned with the crease, press the point and then press out the crease line too.

## Assemble Dresden Plate

*It is imperative that the petal seams are a scant ¼" or the plate will not lie flat. For illustrated guidance, refer to Setting up Your Machine with a Perfect Piecing Seam Guide (page 12). For detailed instructions on neatly sewing together petals, refer to Stitching Petal to Petal Without Leaving Thread Tails (page 19).*

**1.** Sew together petals in pairs starting 3 stitches from the edge of the petals, backstitching, and then sewing the seam. Make 6 pairs.

**2.** Press each seam flat (as it was sewn) to set the stitches, then press it open.

Don't trim these seams.

**3.** Verify that your seams are a scant ¼" by using the illustrations in Check Your Sewing Accuracy (page 20).

**4.** Sew together 2 pairs of petals. Press each seam to set, then press open. Make 3 sections.

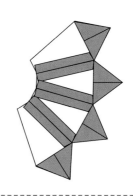

**5.** Sew together 3 sections to complete a plate. Press the 3 seams flat to set, then press them open. Spray the front and wrong sides of the plate with Mary Ellen's Best Press, and press the plate again.

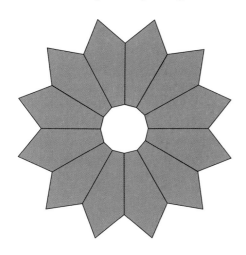

## STITCHING PETAL TO PETAL WITHOUT LEAVING THREAD TAILS

There are no little thread tails at the edges of my Dresden plates. Yours will look just as tidy if you follow these steps, starting each seam about 3 stitches in from the edge.

**1.** Align 2 petals. Lower the needle along the scant ¼" seam allowance, but in from the edge of the petals approximately ³⁄₁₆".

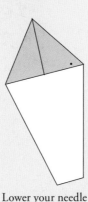

Lower your needle at the dot.

**2.** Backstitch to the edge of the petals.

**3.** Sew the entire seam.

**4.** Trim the thread tails.

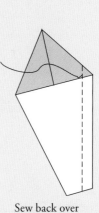

Sew back over a few of the original stitches.

# CHECK YOUR SEWING ACCURACY

**1.** Use these illustrations to gauge your seam accuracy. Place sewn pairs of petals over these illustrations to be sure you are sewing exact scant ¼″ seams. If your petals do not fit the diagrams, adjust the seam allowance.

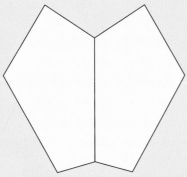

2 Tiny Dresden petals should fit this perfectly.

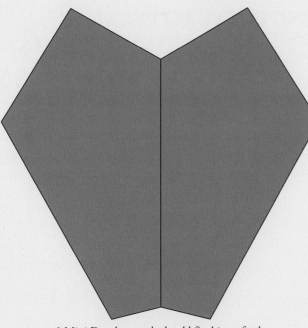

2 Mini Dresden petals should fit this perfectly.

**2.** If your petals are bigger than the diagram, increase your seam allowance. If your petals are smaller than the diagram, reduce your seam allowance.

## Make the Center

*Trace the included circle patterns (page 86) or use paper circle cutters to make templates for making the centers.*

**1.** For a Tiny Dresden plate, cut a square of freezer paper 1½″ × 1½″ or for a Mini Dresden plate, cut a square of freezer paper 2½″ × 2½″. Trace the appropriate circle onto the paper and cut out the circle.

### Tip: Six at Once Saves Time

When making multiple blocks, cut out 6 circles at once. Put 6 freezer paper squares into a circle cutter or staple together 6 paper squares with a traced circle on the top sheet. Cut out all the layers at once.

**2.** Press the waxy side of a circle template to the wrong side of the Dresden center fabric square leaving at least ¼″ all around.

**3.** Cut out the circle adding ¼″ seam allowance.

**4.** Glue the seam allowance to the paper side of the template using Roxanne, or another fabric glue and the APLIQUICK bars.

**5.** Glue the edge of the circle to the center of the plate.

**6.** Appliqué the center circle to the plate using a thread color that matches the center circle fabric. For detailed instructions, refer to the Blind Hem Appliqué Stitch (page 21).

**7.** Dampen the center circle by running a little water over it and working the water into the fabric with your fingers. Let it rest a few minutes, then remove the paper template through the hole in the back. Give a gentle pull diagonally on the plate to release the paper.

**8.** Let the plate dry, then spray it with Mary Ellen's Best Press, and iron.

### Tip: Caution

Pressing plates while they're still wet will distort them. Let them dry!

# BLIND HEM APPLIQUÉ STITCH

Use your machine's blind hem stitch for sewing the center circles onto Dresden plates and for stitching the plates onto the background fabric. The appliqué stitches will be practically invisible and resemble hand stitching.

**1.** Set your machine for a blind hem stitch.

**2.** Adjust the stitch width so it is very narrow. (The needle should move just a few threads to the left.) Set the stitch length so it is very short. (Each short row of straight stitches should measure between ⅛″ and ³⁄₁₆″.)

## Tip

**If your machine does not allow you to alter the stitch length or width when making a blind hem stitch, try using a small zigzag, another pre-programmed stitch, or hand stitch the plates instead.**

**3.** Practice the stitch on scraps until you're pleased with the results. You will have a few tiny stitches forward, and then a zigzag stitch to the left. Use a thread color that matches the piece being appliquéd down.

Match your thread color; the sample shows a contrasting color to make it easier to see the stitching.

## Appliqué Plate to Background Fabric

**1.** Fold and press the Tiny Dresden background square 5″ × 5″ or the Mini Dresden background square 9½″ × 9½″ in half in both directions to create crease lines for centering the plate.

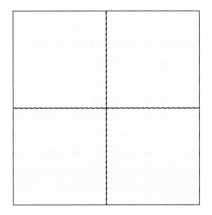

**2.** Glue the plate to the background square by applying a bead of glue around the outer edge on the back of the plate, then aligning the plate with the creases on the background square.

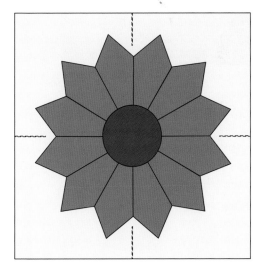

**3.** Appliqué the plate to the background square using thread that matches the petals and the same method that was used to appliqué the centers. For multiple colors of petals, use a neutral thread color such as Sulky 733-1180.

## Tip: No Need to Trim

**Leave the background fabric in place behind your Dresden plates to give extra stability to your little blocks.**

# Sharing My Happy

Fabric choices can really change the look of a quilt. The sophisticated paisley reproduction print used as over-sized sashing in this quilt creates a lot of movement as well as pattern. Using calmer background prints for the blocks makes the Tiny Dresden plates really pop!

Quilted by Tamara Lynn

## Materials

**Background #1:** ⅔ yard for purple Dresden plates and sawtooth border

**Background #2:** ⅓ yard for pink Dresden plates

**Pink:** ⅓ yard for Dresden petals

**Purples (6):** ¼ yard of each purple fabric for Dresden petals and sawtooth border

**Sashing:** ½ yard

**Binding:** ⅓ yard

**Backing:** 1¼ yards

**Batting:** 43″ × 43″

**Freezer paper**

**Fabric glue:** Such as Roxanne Glue-Baste-It

**Thread:** To match fabrics

**That Purple Thang**

**Mary Ellen's Best Press:** In single-finger pump bottle

**Thangles:** For 1½″ finished half-square triangles (recommended)

**Templates:** Suzn Quilts' Tiny Dresden Plate Template #216 (highly recommended)

**Paper cutter:** 1″ circle (recommended)

## Cutting

*Before cutting, lightly spray each fabric with Mary Ellen's Best Press then iron dry as instructed in Best Press Dos and Don'ts (page 12). To cut petal shapes, use Suzn Quilts' Tiny Dresden Template #216 or the Tiny Dresden petal pattern (page 86). Please note the alternate cutting instructions if you are using Thangles to make half-square triangles.*

### Background #1

- Cut 2 strips 5″ × width of fabric; subcut into 16 squares 5″ × 5″.

- Cut 3 strips 2½″ × width of fabric; subcut into 42 squares 2½″ × 2½″. *Or, if using Thangles, cut 4 strips 2″ × width of fabric instead.*

### Background #2

- Cut 2 strips 5″ × width of fabric; subcut into 9 squares 5″ × 5″.

### Pink

- Cut 4 strips 2″ × width of fabric; subcut into 108 petals.

### Purples (6)

*To achieve a scrappy look, the distribution of purple fabrics used to sew plates and half-square triangles won't be even. Choose how much you cut from each of your purples so that you have the totals listed below. When assembling your plates, note that each is made with petals from a single print.*

- Cut 16 strips 2″ × 16″ (total); subcut into 12 petals each to make 192 petals total.

- Cut 4 squares 2″ × 2″.

- Cut 3 strips 2½″ × width of fabric; subcut into 42 squares 2½″ × 2½″. *Or, if using Thangles, cut 4 strips 2″ × width of fabric instead.*

### Sashing

- Cut 3 strips 5″ × width of fabric; subcut into 12 rectangles 5″ × 9½″.

### Binding

- Cut 4 strips 2½″ × width of fabric.

### Freezer paper

- Cut 25 squares 1½″ × 1½″.

# Construction

*Seam allowances are scant ¼" unless otherwise noted.*

## Tiny Dresden Plates

*For detailed instructions, refer to Tiny and Mini Dresden Plate Assembly Techniques (page 16).*

**1.** Assemble 9 Tiny Dresden plates using the 108 pink Tiny Dresden petals.

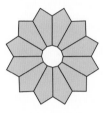

**2.** Make 9 purple 1″ centers and appliqué them to the pink Dresden plates.

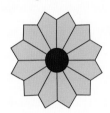

**3.** Remove the freezer paper templates and let the completed plates dry. Once dry, iron them with Best Press.

**Tip: Be Patient!**

**Let your plates dry. Pressing plates while they're still wet distorts them.**

**4.** Appliqué each pink Dresden plate to a Background #2 square 5″ × 5″.

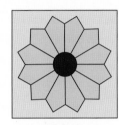

Make 9.

**5.** Assemble 16 Tiny Dresden plates using the 192 purple Tiny Dresden petals. Make each plate using 12 petals of the *same* purple fabric.

**6.** Make 16 pink 1″ centers and appliqué them to the purple Dresden plates.

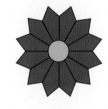

**7.** Remove the freezer paper templates and let the completed plates dry. Once dry, press them again with Best Press.

**8.** Appliqué each purple Dresden plate to a Background #1 square 5″ × 5″.

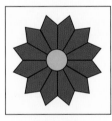

Make 16.

**9.** Sew together 4 purple Tiny Dresden blocks to make a Four-Patch block.

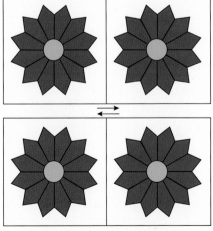

Press seams in opposite directions as shown by arrows.

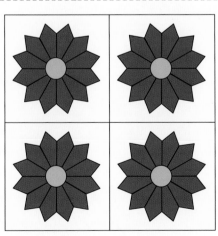

Four-Patch block; make 4.

# Quilt Top

1. Sew together 2 sashing rectangles 5″ × 9½″ and 3 pink Tiny Dresden blocks, alternating the sashing and blocks. Press the seams toward the sashing.

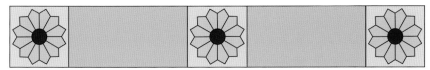

Make 3.

2. Sew together 3 sashing rectangles 5″ × 9½″ and 2 purple Four-Patch blocks, alternating the sashing and blocks. Press the seams toward the sashing.

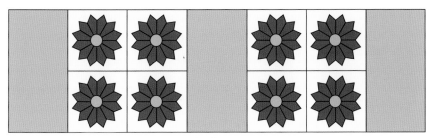

Make 2.

3. Sew together the rows and press the seams away from the purple Dresden plate rows.

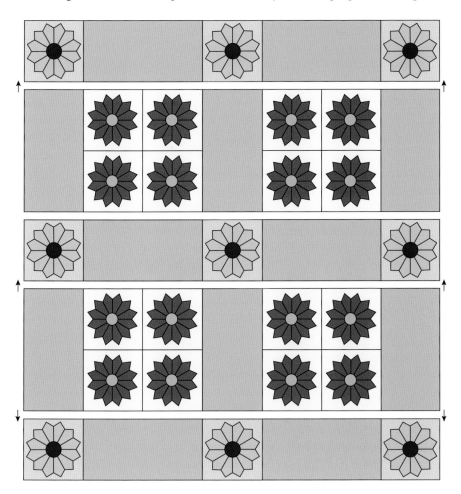

# Sawtooth Border Strips

## HALF-SQUARE TRIANGLES

*If using Thangles, follow the manufacturer's instructions for 1½" finished size and make 84 half-square triangles, skipping Steps 1–3.*

**1.** Place a Background #1 square 2½" × 2½" on top of a purple square 2½" × 2½" with right sides together.

**2.** Draw a diagonal line across Background #1 square. Stitch a scant ¼" on both sides of that line.

**3.** Cut apart the squares directly along the drawn line. Press the seams toward the purple triangles. Trim each to a 2" × 2" square.

Half-square triangle; make 84.

**4.** Sew 21 half-square triangles into a border strip, noting the direction of the triangles. Press the seams toward the purple triangles.

Sawtooth border strip; make 4.

**5.** Sew purple squares 2" × 2" onto the ends of 2 border strips and press the seams toward the purple squares. These are the top and bottom border strips.

Make 2.

**6.** Sew the side border strips onto the quilt, then attach the top and bottom strips, pressing after each addition.

# Finishing

**1.** Layer the completed top with backing and batting.

**2.** Quilt, bind, and label.

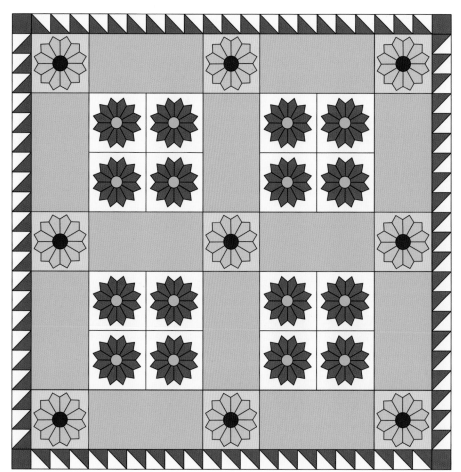

*Sharing My Happy* quilt assembly

# A Blooming Day

Enjoy beautiful Tiny Dresden plates every day with this table runner on display!

Quilted by Tamara Lynn

## Materials

**Cream:** ⅓ yard for block background

**Black:** ⅓ yard for Dresden plate background

**Green:** ½ yard for blocks and binding

**Pink #1:** ¼ yard for Dresden petals

**Pink #2:** ¼ yard for Dresden petals

**Yellow:** Scrap for Dresden plate centers

**Backing:** 1⅓ yards

**Batting:** 21″ × 47″

**Freezer paper**

**Fabric glue:** Such as Roxanne Glue-Baste-It

**Thread:** To match fabrics

**That Purple Thang**

**Mary Ellen's Best Press:** In single-finger pump bottle

**Templates:** Suzn Quilts' Tiny Dresden Plate Template #216 (highly recommended)

**Paper cutter:** 1″ circle (recommended)

## Cutting

*Before cutting, lightly spray each fabric with Mary Ellen's Best Press then iron dry as instructed in Best Press Dos and Don'ts (page 12). To cut petal shapes, use Suzn Quilts' Tiny Dresden Template #216 or the Tiny Dresden petal pattern (page 86).*

### Cream

- Cut 3 strips 2¾″ × width of fabric; subcut into 12 rectangles 2¾″ × 5″ and 12 squares 2¾″ × 2¾″.

### Black

- Cut 1 strip 5″ × width of fabric; subcut into 7 squares 5″ × 5″.

- Cut 1 strip 4½″ × width of fabric; subcut into 4 squares 4½″ × 4½″. Subcut the 4½″ × 4½″ squares twice diagonally. Trim remainder of strip to 3¼″; subcut into 4 squares 3¼″ × 3¼″.

### Green

- Cut 1 strip 3¼″ × width of fabric; subcut into 4 squares 3¼″ × 3¼″. Trim remainder of strip to 2¾″; subcut into 9 squares 2¾″ × 2¾″.

- Cut 1 strip 2¾″ × width of fabric; subcut into 15 squares 2¾″ × 2¾″ (24 total).

- Cut 3 strips 2½″ × width of fabric for binding.

### Pink #1

- Cut 2 strips 2″ × width of fabric; subcut into 36 Tiny Dresden petals.

### Pink #2

- Cut 2 strips 2″ × width of fabric; subcut into 48 Tiny Dresden petals.

### Freezer paper

- Cut 7 squares 1½″ × 1½″.

# Construction

*Seam allowances are scant ¼″ unless noted.*

## Tiny Dresden Plates

*For detailed instructions, refer to Tiny and Mini Dresden Plate Assembly Techniques (page 16).*

**1.** Assemble 7 Tiny Dresden plates using the 84 pink Tiny Dresden petals. Make each plate using 12 petals of the same pink fabric.

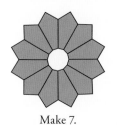

Make 7.

**2.** Make 7 yellow 1″ centers and appliqué them to the Tiny Dresden plates.

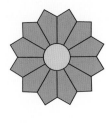

**3.** Remove the freezer paper templates and let the completed plates dry. Once dry, iron them with Best Press.

**Tip: Be Patient!**

Let your plates dry. Pressing plates while they're still wet distorts them.

**4.** Appliqué the Tiny Dresden plates to the 5″ × 5″ black squares.

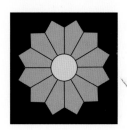

Make 7.

## Dresden Eight-Pointed Star Blocks

*The unfinished block will measure 9½″ × 9½″.*

### FLYING GEESE

**1.** Place a green square 2¾″ × 2¾″ on top of a cream rectangle 2¾″ × 5″, with right sides together.

**2.** Draw a diagonal line across the green square. Stitch on the line and then trim the seam allowance to ¼″.

**3.** Press the seam flat first and then press it toward the green fabric.

**4.** Repeat Steps 1–3 using another green square 2¾″ × 2¾″ on the opposite corner. Trim, then press.

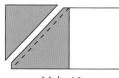

Make 12.

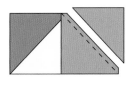

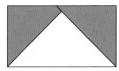

Flying Geese; make 12.

### ASSEMBLE THE BLOCKS

Sew together 4 Flying Geese, 4 cream squares 2¾″ × 2¾″, and 1 pink #1 Tiny Dresden plate block as shown. Press the seams in the direction of the arrows.

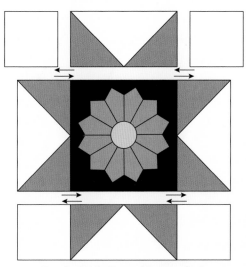

Dresden Eight-Pointed Star; make 3.

## Dresden Filler Blocks

### HALF-SQUARE TRIANGLES

**1.** Place a green square 3¼″ × 3¼″ on top of a black square 3¼″ × 3¼″, with right sides together.

**2.** Draw a diagonal line across the green square. Stitch a scant ¼″ on both sides of that line.

**3.** Cut apart along the drawn line. Press the same to set, then press towards the black fabric. Trim each to a 2¾″ × 2¾″ square.

Half-square triangle; make 8.

### TRIANGLE BLOCKS

**1.** Sew together a half-square triangle and 2 black 4½″ quarter-cut triangles as shown. Press the seams away from the half-square triangle.

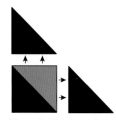

Triangle block; make 8.

**2.** Sew 2 triangle blocks with a pink #2 Tiny Dresden Block. Press the seams toward the Tiny Dresden block.

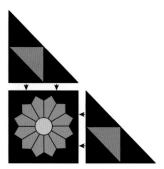

Dresden filler block; make 4.

## Assemble the Table Runner

**1.** Sew the Eight-Pointed Star blocks and the filler blocks into rows as shown. Press open the seams.

**2.** Sew the rows together to complete the table runner. Press open the seams.

*A Blooming Day* quilt assembly

## Finishing

**1.** Layer the completed top with backing and batting.

**2.** Quilt, bind, and label.

# Argyle Retreat

**Finished blocks:** 4½″ × 4½″ and 13½″ × 13½″

**Finished quilt:** 68″ × 95″

The secondary pattern made by the Tiny Dresdens in this quilt reminds me of argyle. Whether we realize it or not, we're constantly influenced by what we see. It's very apparent in children. Typically they mimic the most silly or outrageous things they see (and often at inopportune times). When I look at things, I often notice patterns, and I frequently insert Dresden plates into them. It can happen at inopportune times for me too—staring too intently at a lady's blouse at church because I see a pattern that would make a nice quilt.

This project is perfect for taking along to a retreat. Once the cutting is done, it's easy to sit and sew without worry of being too distracted. I speak from experience, having pieced this quilt while on a retreat with my quilting friends!

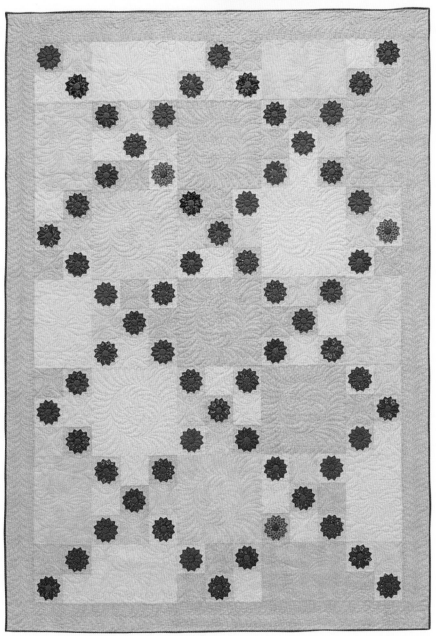

Quilted by Tamara Lynn

## Materials

**Cream background:** 6 yards (more yardage may be required if using multiple fabrics)

**Teals (6):** ⅓ yard of each fabric for Tiny Dresden plates

**Olive green:** ¼ yard for Tiny Dresden centers

**Binding:** ⅔ yard

**Backing:** 6 yards

**Batting:** 78″ × 105″

**Freezer paper**

**Fabric glue:** Such as Roxanne Glue-Baste-It

**Thread:** To match fabrics

**That Purple Thang**

**Mary Ellen's Best Press:** In single-finger pump bottle

**Templates:** Suzn Quilts' Tiny Dresden Plate Template #216 (highly recommended)

**Paper cutter:** 1″ circle (highly recommended)

## Cutting

*Before cutting, lightly spray each fabric with Mary Ellen's Best Press then iron dry as instructed in Best Press Dos and Don'ts (page 12). To cut petal shapes, use Suzn Quilts' Tiny Dresden Template #216 or the Tiny Dresden petal pattern (page 86).*

### Cream background

• Cut 6 strips 14″ × width of fabric; subcut into 7 squares 14″ × 14″, 10 rectangles 9½″ × 14″, 14 squares 5″ × 5″.

• Cut 22 strips 5″ × width of fabric; piece strips to make 2 borders 5″ × 68″, 2 borders 5″ × 86″, and 110 squares 5″ × 5″.

### Teals (6)

*From each fabric:*

• Cut 5 strips 2″ × width of fabric (30 total); subcut 132 Tiny Dresden petals each (792 petals total).

### Binding

• Cut 8 strips 2½″ × width of fabric for binding.

### Freezer paper

• Cut 66 squares 1½″ × 1½″.

# Construction

*Seam allowances are scant ¼″ unless noted.*

## Tiny Dresden Blocks

*For detailed instructions, refer to Tiny and Mini Dresden Plate Assembly Techniques (page 16).*

**1.** Assemble 66 Tiny Dresden plates using the 792 Tiny Dresden teal petals. Make each plate using 12 petals of the *same* teal fabric. There will be 11 plates of each fabric (if you are using 6 different teal fabrics).

**2.** Make 66 olive green 1″ centers and appliqué them to the Tiny Dresden plates.

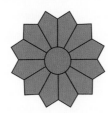

**3.** Remove the freezer paper templates and let the completed plates dry. Once dry, iron them with Best Press.

**Tip: Be Patient!**

Let your plates dry. Pressing plates while they're still wet distorts them.

**4.** Appliqué each Tiny Dresden plate to a cream background square 5″ × 5″.

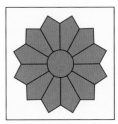

Make 66.

## Assemble the Blocks

**1.** Sew together 5 Tiny Dresden blocks and 4 cream background squares 5″ × 5″ to make a Nine-Patch block. Press the seams away from the Tiny Dresden blocks.

Nine-Patch block; make 8.

**2.** Sew together 3 Tiny Dresden blocks and 3 cream background squares 5″ × 5″ to make a Six-Patch block.

Six-Patch block; make 6.

**3.** Sew together 2 Tiny Dresden blocks and 2 cream background squares 5″ × 5″ to make a Four-Patch block.

Four-Patch block; make 4.

## Assemble the Quilt

**1.** Sew together 2 Four-Patch blocks, 1 Six-Patch block, and 2 cream background rectangles 9½″ × 14″ as shown. Press the seams toward the cream background rectangles.

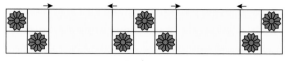

Make 2.

**2.** Sew together 2 Six-Patch blocks, 1 Nine-Patch block, and 2 cream background squares 14″ × 14″ as shown. Press the seams toward the cream background squares.

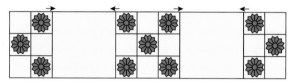

Make 2.

**3.** Sew together 2 Nine-Patch blocks, 2 cream background rectangles 9½″ × 14″, and 1 cream background square 14″ × 14″ as shown. Press the seams toward the cream background square and rectangle.

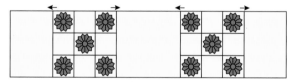

Make 3.

**4.** Sew the rows together and press the seams as you prefer. Next, sew the side border strips onto the quilt and press. Finally, sew the top and bottom border strips onto the quilt and press.

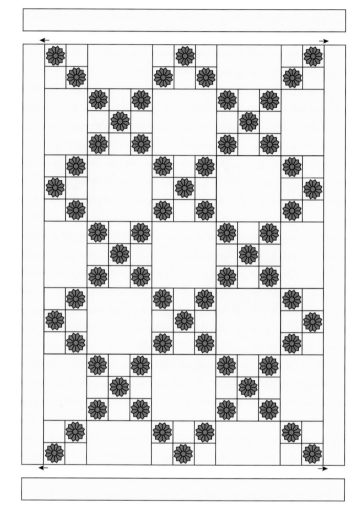

*Argyle Retreat* quilt assembly

## Finishing

**1.** Layer the completed top with backing and batting.

**2.** Quilt, bind, and label.

# Widgets

**Finished block:** 9″ × 9″
**Finished quilt:** 20½″ × 20½″

Looking for a fun little quilt to whet your Dresden appetite without biting off more than you can chew? Eureka, you have found it! Make both Tiny and Mini Dresdens and practice your machine quilting skills on this winning little quilt.

Quilted by Tamara Lynn

## Materials

**Cream:** ½ yard for block background and sawtooth border

**Yellow:** ¼ yard for block background

**Blue:** ¼ yard for Dresden petals, Dresden center and corner stones

**Red:** ¼ yard for Dresden petals, Dresden centers and sawtooth border

**Green:** ⅓ yard for Dresden petals and binding

**Backing:** ⅞ yard

**Batting:** 29″ × 29″

**Freezer paper**

**Fabric glue:** Such as Roxanne Glue-Baste-It

**Thread:** To match fabrics

**That Purple Thang**

**Mary Ellen's Best Press:**
In single-finger pump bottle

**Templates:**

• Suzn Quilts' Tiny Dresden Plate Template #216 (recommended)

• Suzn Quilts' Mini Dresden Plate Template #186 (recommended)

**Paper cutters:**

• 1″ circle (recommended)

• 2″ circle (recommended)

**Thangles:** For 1″ finished half-square triangles (highly recommended)

## Cutting

*Before cutting, lightly spray each fabric with Mary Ellen's Best Press then iron dry as instructed in Best Press Dos and Don'ts (page 12). To cut petal shapes, use Suzn Quilts' Tiny Dresden Template #216 and Mini Dresden Template #186 or the Tiny and Mini Dresden petal patterns (page 86). Please note the alternate cutting instructions if you are using Thangles to make half-square triangles.*

### Cream

• Cut 1 strip 5″ × width of fabric; subcut into 8 squares 5″ × 5″.

• Cut 2 strips 2″ × width of fabric; subcut into 36 squares 2″ × 2″. *Or, if using Thangles*, cut 2 strips 1½″ × width of fabric instead.

### Yellow

• Cut 1 strip 5″ × width of fabric; subcut into 8 squares 5″ × 5″.

### Blue

• Cut 1 strip 2″ × width of fabric; subcut into 24 Tiny Dresden petals.

• Cut 4 squares 1½″ × 1½″.

### Red

• Cut 1 strip 2″ × width of fabric; subcut into 12 Tiny Dresden petals.

• Cut 2 strips 2″ × width of fabric; subcut into 36 squares 2″ × 2″. *Or, if using Thangles*, cut 2 strips 1½″ × width of fabric instead.

### Green

• Cut 1 strip 3½″ × width of fabric; subcut into 24 Mini Dresden petals.

• Cut 3 strips 2½″ × width of fabric for binding.

### Freezer paper

• Cut 1 square 1½″ × 1½″.

• Cut 4 squares 2½″ × 2½″.

# Construction

*Seam allowances are scant ¼″ unless noted.*

## Tiny Dresden and Mini Dresden Plates

*For detailed instructions, refer to Tiny and Mini Dresden Plate Assembly Techniques (page 16).*

**1.** Assemble 8 Tiny Dresden quarter plates using the 24 blue petals and sewing them together in sets of 3.

Blue quarter plate; make 8.

**2.** Assemble 1 Tiny Dresden plate using the 12 red petals and set it aside.

Red Tiny Dresden plate; make 1.

**3.** Assemble 8 Mini Dresden quarter plates using the 24 green petals and sewing them together in sets of 3.

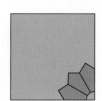

Green quarter plate; make 8.

**4.** Appliqué 4 blue Tiny Dresden quarter plates onto the corners of 4 cream squares 5″ × 5″ and the remaining 4 blue Tiny Dresden quarter plates onto the corners of 4 yellow squares 5″ × 5″.

Make 4 of each.

**5.** Appliqué 4 green Mini Dresden quarter plates onto the corners of 4 cream squares 5″ × 5″ and the remaining 4 green Mini Dresden quarter plates onto the corners of 4 yellow squares 5″ × 5″.

Make 4 of each.

## Assemble the Blocks

**1.** Sew together 2 Tiny Dresden blue-on-cream squares with 2 Mini Dresden green-on-yellow squares as shown. Press the seam allowances toward the yellow squares.

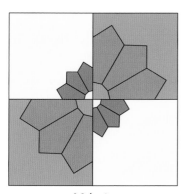

Make 2.

**2.** Sew together 2 Tiny Dresden blue-on-yellow squares with 2 Mini Dresden green-on-cream squares as shown. Press the seam allowances toward the yellow squares.

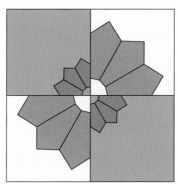

Make 2.

**3.** Make 4 red 2″ centers and appliqué them to the blocks.

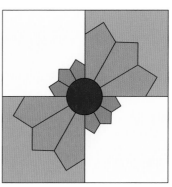

Make 4.

**4.** Make 1 blue 1″ center and appliqué it to the center of the red Tiny Dresden plate.

Make 1.

**5.** Remove the freezer paper templates, and then let the completed plate dry. Note, you'll need to carefully cut a slit in the background fabric behind each Dresden plate to remove the paper template. Once dry, iron them with Best Press.

### Tip: Be Patient!

Let your plates dry. Pressing plates while they're still wet distorts them.

## Assemble the Quilt

**1.** Sew together the 4 blocks as shown.

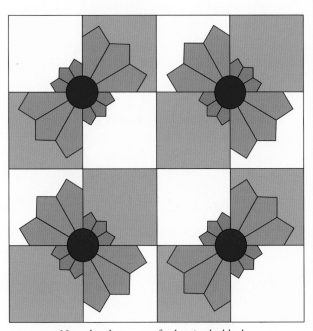

Note the placement of colors in the blocks.

**2.** Appliqué the red Tiny Dresden plate to the center of the quilt.

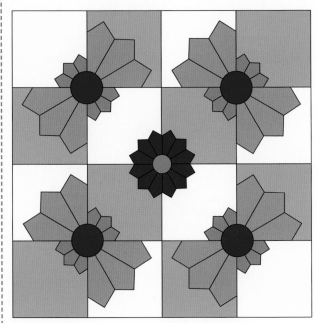

# Sawtooth Border Strips

## HALF-SQUARE TRIANGLES

*If using Thangles, follow the manufacturer's instructions for 1" finished size and make 72 half-square triangles, skipping Steps 1–3.*

**1.** Place a cream square 2" × 2" on top of a red square 2" × 2" with right sides together.

**2.** Draw a diagonal line across the cream square. Stitch a scant ¼" on both sides of the line.

**3.** Cut along the drawn line. Press the seams toward the red triangles. Trim each to a 1½" × 1½" square.

Half-square triangle; make 72.

**4.** Sew 18 half-square triangles into a border strip, noting the direction of the triangles. Press the seams toward the red triangles.

Sawtooth border strip; make 4.

**5.** Sew blue squares 1½" × 1½" to the ends of 2 border strips and press the seams toward the blue squares. These are the top and bottom border strips.

Make 2.

**6.** Sew the side border strips onto the quilt, then attach the top and bottom strips, pressing with each addition.

# Finishing

**1.** Layer the completed top with backing and batting.

**2.** Quilt, bind, and label.

*Widgets* quilt assembly

# Cross Roads

**Finished block:** 4½″ × 4½″
**Finished quilt:** 32″ × 32″

The more fabrics I can use in one quilt, the happier I am. Sure, you can use just one purple fabric in this quilt. And you can use just one olive green and background print, but where's the fun in that? Add dimension and movement by choosing a couple fabrics for each. Otherwise, you might end up feeling jealous when my quilt is prettier than yours … just sayin'!

Quilted by Tamara Lynn

## Materials

**Cream #1:** ⅓ yard for Tiny Dresden background and Nine-Patch blocks

**Cream #2:** ½ yard for Nine-Patch blocks

**Cream #3:** ⅓ yard for Mini Dresden background and Nine-Patch blocks

**Purple #1:** ⅓ yard for Nine-Patch blocks

**Purple #2:** ⅔ yard for Tiny Dresden petals, Mini Dresden petals, and binding

**Olive green #1:** Scrap for Tiny Dresden and Mini Dresden centers

**Olive green #2:** ⅔ yard for border

**Backing:** 1 yard

**Batting:** 40″ × 40″

**Freezer paper**

**Fabric glue:** Such as Roxanne Glue-Baste-It

**Thread:** To match fabrics

**That Purple Thang**

**Mary Ellen's Best Press:** In single-finger pump bottle

**Templates:**

- Suzn Quilts' Tiny Dresden Plate Template #216 (highly recommended)

- Suzn Quilts' Mini Dresden Plate Template #816 (highly recommended)

**Paper cutters:**

- 1″ circle (recommended)

- 2″ circle (recommended)

## Cutting

*Before cutting, lightly spray each fabric with Mary Ellen's Best Press then iron dry as instructed in Best Press Dos and Don'ts (page 12). To cut petal shapes, use Suzn Quilts' Tiny Dresden Template #216 and Mini Dresden Template #186 or the Tiny and Mini Dresden petal patterns (page 86).*

### Cream #1

- Cut 1 strip 5″ × width of fabric; subcut into 5 squares 5″ × 5″.

- Cut 1 strip 2″ × 33″.

### Cream #2

- Cut 6 strips 2″ × width of fabric; subcut into:

  2 strips 2″ × 41″

  1 strip 2″ × 33″

  3 strips 2″ × 25″

  1 strip 2″ × 17″

  2 strips 2″ × 9″

### Cream #3

- Cut 3 strips 2″ × width of fabric; subcut into:

  1 strip 2″ × 41″

  2 strips 2″ × 25″

  1 strip 2″ × 9″

### Purple #1

- Cut 3 strips 2″ × width of fabric; subcut into:

  1 strip 2″ × 33″

  1 strip 2″ × 25″

  2 strips 2″ × 17″

### Purple #2

- Cut 1 strip 3½″ × width of fabric; subcut into 12 Mini Dresden petals.

- Cut 2 strip 2″ × width of fabric. Cut 48 Tiny Dresden petals.

### Olive green #2

- Cut 4 strips 5″ × 23″.

### Binding

- Cut 4 strips 2½″ × width of fabric.

### Freezer paper

- Cut 4 squares 1½″ × 1½″.

- Cut 1 square 2½″ × 2½″.

# Construction

*Seam allowances are scant ¼″ unless noted.*

## Tiny Dresden Plates

*For detailed instructions, refer to Tiny and Mini Dresden Plate Assembly Techniques (page 16).*

**1.** Assemble 4 Tiny Dresden plates using the 48 Tiny Dresden petals.

**2.** Assemble 1 Mini Dresden plate using the 12 Mini Dresden petals.

**3.** Make 4 olive green 1″ centers and appliqué them to the Tiny Dresden plates.

**4.** Make 1 olive green 2″ center and appliqué it to the Mini Dresden plate.

**5.** Remove the freezer-paper templates and let the completed plates dry. Once dry, iron them with Best Press.

### Tip: Be Patient!

**Let your plates dry. Pressing plates while they're still wet distorts them.**

**6.** Appliqué the Tiny Dresden plate to a cream #1 square 5″ × 5″. Repeat to make 4.

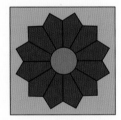

Tiny Dresden block; make 4.

## Nine-Patch Blocks

**STRIP SETS**

**1.** Sew a cream #3 strip 2″ × 9″ between 2 cream #2 strips 2″ × 9″, with right sides together. Press the seams flat to set, then press toward the cream #2 strips.

**2.** Sew a cream #3 strip 2″ × 41″ between 2 cream #2 strips 2″ × 41″, with right sides together. Press the seams flat to set, then press toward cream #2 strips.

**3.** Cut the strip set from Steps 1 and 2 into 2″ segments.

Segment A; cut 24.

**4.** Sew a cream #2 strip 2″ × 25″ right sides together between 2 cream #3 strips 2″ × 25″. Press the seams flat to set, then press toward the cream #2 strips.

**5.** Cut the strip set from Step 4 into 2″ segments.

Segment B; cut 12.

**6.** Sew a purple #1 strip 2″ × 25″ between 2 cream #2 strips 2″ × 25″, with right sides together. Press the seams flat to set, then press toward the cream #2 strips.

**7.** Cut the strip set from Step 6 into 2″ segments.

Segment C; cut 12.

**8.** Sew a cream #2 strip 2″ × 17″ between 2 purple #1 strips 2″ × 17″, with right sides together. Press the seams flat to set, then press toward cream #2 strip.

**9.** Cut the strip set from Step 8 into 2″ segments.

Segment D; cut 8.

**10.** Sew a cream #2 strip 2″ × 33″ between a cream #1 strip 2″ × 33″ and a purple #1 strip 2″ × 33″, with right sides together. Press the seams flat to set, and then press toward the cream #2 strip.

**11.** Cut the strip set from Step 10 into 2″ segments.

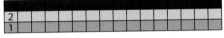
Segment E; cut 16.

## ASSEMBLE THE BLOCKS

**1.** Sew a Segment B between 2 Segment A's, with right sides together. *Don't press these seams until you sew the block into the quilt and can alter the direction of the seams as needed.*

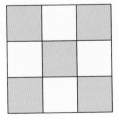
Make 12.

**2.** Sew a Segment C right sides together between 2 Segment E's. *Don't press these seams until you sew the block into the quilt and can alter the direction of the seams as needed.*

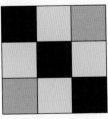
Make 8.

**3.** Sew a Segment C right sides together between 2 Segment D's. I don't press these seams until I sew the block into the quilt so I can alter the seam direction, as I get ready to sew it into the quilt.

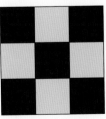
Make 4.

## Assemble the Quilt

1. Sew the Nine-Patch blocks and the remaining cream #1 square 5″ × 5″ into rows as shown, pinning at each seam. Press.

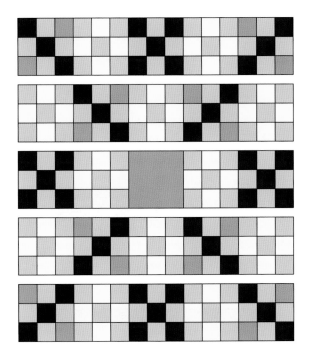

2. Sew Tiny Dresden blocks to the ends of 2 olive green border strips 5″ × 23″. Press the seams toward the green fabric.

Top and bottom border strips; make 2.

3. Sew 2 olive green 5″ × 23″ side border strips onto the quilt. Press the seams toward the olive green border strips.

4. Sew the top and bottom border strips onto the quilt.

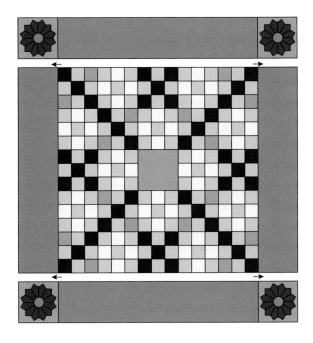

5. Glue the Mini Dresden plate onto the center of the quilt and then appliqué it in place.

*Cross Roads* quilt assembly

## Finishing

1. Layer the completed top with backing and batting.

2. Quilt, bind, and label.

# Star-Spangled Dresdens

**Finished block:** 12″ × 12″

**Finished quilt:** 35″ × 35″

Quite often, the quilt that I just finished is my new favorite. But every time I look at this quilt, I love the way the Tiny Dresdens look so at home inside the stars. It makes me smile and I can't wait to hang it on my wall for the 4th of July. In fact, I like it so much that I'm wondering what it will look like made with other colors.

Quilted by Tamara Lynn

## Materials

**Cream:** 1⅛ yards for background

**Blue:** ⅔ yard for blocks and outer border

**Red:** ⅔ yard for blocks and Dresden petals

**Black:** ⅔ yard for sashing, binding, and Dresden centers

**Backing:** 1¼ yards

**Batting:** 43″ × 43″

**Freezer paper**

**Fabric glue:** Such as Roxanne Glue-Baste-It

**Thread:** To match fabrics

**That Purple Thang**

**Mary Ellen's Best Press:** In single-finger pump bottle

**Templates:** Suzn Quilts' Tiny Dresden Plate Template #216 (highly recommended)

**Paper cutter:** 1″ circle (recommended)

## Cutting

*Before cutting, lightly spray each fabric with Mary Ellen's Best Press then iron dry as instructed in Best Press Dos and Don'ts (page 12). To cut petal shapes, use Suzn Quilts' Tiny Dresden Template #216 or the Tiny Dresden petal pattern (page 86).*

### Cream

• Cut 4 strips 3½″ × width of fabric; subcut into 16 rectangles 3½″ × 6½″ and 16 squares 3½″ × 3½″.

• Cut 4 strips 3¼″ × width of fabric; subcut into 2 strips 3¼″ × 27½″ and 2 strips 3¼″ × 33″.

• Cut 2 squares 8¾″ × 8¾″.

### Blue

• Cut 2 strips 3½″ × width of fabric; subcut into 16 squares 3½″ × 3½″.

• Cut 4 strips 1½″ × width of fabric; subcut into 2 strips 1½″ × 33″ and 2 strips 1½″ × 35″.

• Cut 2 squares 8¾″ × 8¾″.

### Red

• Cut 2 strips 3½″ × width of fabric; subcut into 16 squares 3½″ × 3½″.

• Cut 1 strip 1½″ × width of fabric; subcut into 8 squares 1½″ × 1½″.

• Cut 4 strips 2″ × width of fabric for Dresden petals. Subcut 108 Tiny Dresden petals.

### Black

• Cut 4 strips 1½″ × width of fabric; subcut into 1 strip 1½″ × 25½″ and 10 strips 1½″ × 12½″.

• Cut 4 strips 2½″ × width of fabric for binding.

### Freezer paper

• Cut 13 squares 1½″ × 1½″.

# Construction

*Seam allowances are scant ¼″ unless noted.*

## Make the Tiny Dresden Plates and Half-Plates

*For detailed instructions, refer to Tiny and Mini Dresden Plate Assembly Techniques (page 16).*

**1.** Assemble 5 Tiny Dresden plates using 60 Tiny Dresden petals.

**2.** Assemble 8 half–Tiny Dresden plates using 48 Tiny Dresden petals.

**3.** Make 13 black 1″ centers and appliqué them to the Tiny Dresden plates and half plates. (The centers will overhang the edge of the half plates.)

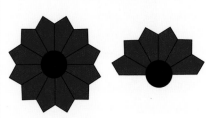

**4.** Trim away the excess black center by cutting along the straight edge of the half plate with a rotary cutter.

Trim away the excess black center.

**5.** Remove the freezer-paper templates, and then let the completed plates dry. Once dry, iron them with Best Press.

**Tip: Be Patient!**

**Let your plates dry. Pressing plates while they're still wet distorts them.**

## Star Blocks

### PINWHEELS

**1.** Place a cream square 8¾″ × 8¾″ on top of a blue square 8¾″ × 8¾″ with right sides together. Draw a diagonal line across the cream square in both directions. Stitch a scant ¼″ on both sides of the line.

**2.** Cut the block down the center both horizontally and vertically.

**3.** Cut apart along the drawn lines.

**4.** Press the seams toward the blue triangles. Trim to 3½″ × 3½″.

Half-square triangle; make 16.

**5.** Repeat Steps 1–4 with the remaining cream and blue squares 8¾″ × 8¾″.

**6.** Sew together pairs of half-square triangles as shown.

Press the seams as indicated by arrows.

**7.** Sew together 2 of these units to make a pinwheel block.

Pinwheel block; make 4.

## FLYING GEESE

**1.** Place a red square 3½″ × 3½″ on top of a cream background rectangle 3½″ × 6½″, with right sides together.

**2.** Draw a diagonal line across the red square. Stitch on that line. Trim away both fabrics ¼″ outside that line. Press the seam to set, and then press toward the red fabric.

**3.** Repeat Steps 1 and 2, adding a blue square 3½″ × 3½″ to the opposite corner of the cream rectangle. Trim, then press.

Flying Geese; make 16.

## ASSEMBLE THE BLOCKS

*The unfinished block will measure 12½″ × 12½″.*

**1.** Sew a Flying Geese between 2 cream squares 3½″ × 3½″. Press the seams away from the Flying Geese. Make 2.

**2.** Sew a Pinwheel between 2 Flying Geese. Press the seams away from the Flying Geese blocks.

**3.** Sew together the 3 rows to complete the block.

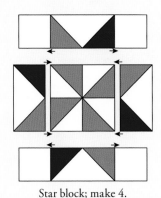

Star block; make 4.

## APPLIQUÉ THE TINY DRESDEN PLATE

Glue a Tiny Dresden plate to the center of each Star block, then appliqué in place.

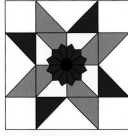

Make 4.

# Assemble the Quilt

**1.** Sew together 2 black strips 1½″ × 12½″ and 3 red squares 1½″ × 1½″ as shown. Press the seams toward the black strips.

Make 2.

**2.** Sew together 1 black strip 1½″ × 25½″ and 2 red squares 1½″ × 1½″.

Make 1.

**3.** Sew together 3 black strips 1½″ × 12½″ and 2 Star Blocks. Press the seams toward the black strips.

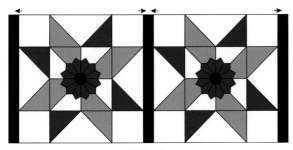

Make 2.

**4.** Sew together the rows. Press the seams toward the black strips.

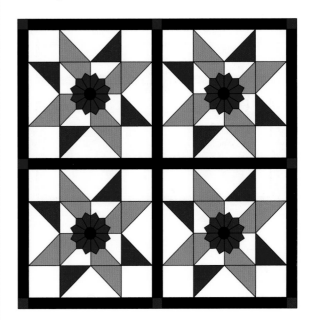

**5.** Glue the remaining Tiny Dresden plate onto the center of the quilt then appliqué in place.

**6.** Glue 2 Tiny Dresden half plates onto the cream strips 3¼″ × 27½″. The centers of the plates should be placed 7¼″ from each end as shown.

7¼″          7¼″

Side borders; make 2.

**7.** Glue 2 Tiny Dresden half plates onto the cream strips 3¼″ × 33″. The centers of the plates should be placed 10″ from each end as shown.

10″          10″

Top and bottom borders; make 2.

**8.** Appliqué the Tiny Dresden half plates in place on the 4 border strips.

**9.** Sew the cream strips 3¼″ × 27½″ onto the sides of the quilt. Press the seams toward the black strips.

**10.** Sew the cream strips 3¼″ × 33″ onto the top and bottom of the quilt. Press the seams toward the black strips.

**11.** Sew the blue strips 1½″ × 33″ onto the sides of the quilt. Press the seams toward the blue strips.

**12.** Sew the blue strips 1½″ × 35″ onto the top and bottom of the quilt. Press the seams towards the blue strips.

*Star-Spangled Dresdens* quilt assembly

## Finishing

**1.** Layer the completed top with backing and batting.

**2.** Quilt, bind, and label.

# Quilt-as-You-Go Button Box

**Finished block:** 4½″ × 4½″

**Finished quilt:** 23″ × 32½″

Some of my best-selling patterns are my quilt-as-you-go designs. The backing and batting are cut to the finished size of the quilt and basted together to act as foundation. The strips are then sewn onto this foundation one at a time. Add the binding and the quilt is done! In this instance, the Tiny Dresden blocks are sewn into strips then the strips are sewn to the foundation. *Button Box* uses charm packs, so a lot of the cutting is already done for you. I love these quilts not only because they're quick and easy, but also because I don't have to figure out *how* to quilt them *or* pay someone else to do it.

## Materials

*Warm and Natural brand cotton batting has "sticky" properties that help ensure the layers stay together during assembly.*

**Charm squares:**

• 25 charm squares 5″ × 5″ for Tiny Dresden block backgrounds

• 50 charm squares 5″ × 5″ for Tiny Dresden petals and centers

**Beige:** ⅓ yard for border

**Red:** ¼ yard for letters

**Binding:** ¼ yard

**Backing:** ¾ yard

**Cotton batting:**
Warm and Natural 25″ × 35″

**Walking foot** (This is a must!)

**Fusible web:** ½ yard

**Thread:** Sulky 12-weight 713-1180 Medium Taupe thread for fusible appliqué

**Quilt basting spray adhesive**

**Masking tape**

**Chaco Liner marking tool**

**Freezer paper**

**Fabric glue:** Such as Roxanne Glue-Baste-It

**That Purple Thang**

**Mary Ellen's Best Press:** In single-finger pump bottle

**Templates:** Suzn Quilts' Tiny Dresden Plate Template #216 (recommended)

**Paper cutter:** 1″ circle (recommended)

**Finger pincushion:** (highly recommended)

## Tip: Master Technique

I'll bet after you make this quilt you'll find that you can do justice to other quilts using the same method. I do not enjoy quilting anything larger than 24″ or so on my home sewing machine, despite taking many machine quilting classes with the best teachers in the field. I send larger quilts to a professional. However, whenever I can quilt-as-I-go, I'm excited. Once the piecing is complete, the quilting is too!

## Cutting

*Before cutting, lightly spray each fabric with Mary Ellen's Best Press, then iron dry as instructed in Best Press Dos and Don'ts (page 12). To cut petal shapes, use Suzn Quilts' Tiny Dresden Template #216 or the Tiny Dresden petal pattern (page 86).*

**Charm squares (50)**

*Cut 6 petals and 1 circle from each charm square carefully, as directed.*

**1.** Cut a 2″ × 5″ strip from 1 charm square.

**2.** *Carefully* cut 6 Tiny Dresden petals and 1 circle 1½″ from the charm square as shown.

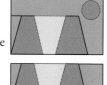

**3.** Repeat Steps 1 and 2 with the remaining 49 charm squares to cut a total of 300 petals.

**Beige**

• Cut 1 strip 10″ × 23″.

**Backing**

• Cut 1 rectangle 23″ × 32½″.

**Binding**

• Cut 3 strips 2½″ × width of fabric.

**Batting**

• Cut 1 rectangle 23″ × 32½″.

**Freezer paper**

• Cut 25 squares 1½″ × 1½″.

# Construction

*Seam allowances are scant ¼" unless noted.*

## Quilt Foundation

*For detailed instructions on basting, refer to Baste the Foundation (below).*

Assemble the quilt foundation by basting together the backing and batting, using spray adhesive or pins.

## BASTE THE FOUNDATION

Use basting spray or pins to baste together the quilt layers when making quilt-as-you-go projects.

### Spray Baste

Basting spray is my favorite basting method. It's quick to apply and there are no pins to remove when sewing. I never spray this in my house because of fumes and overspray. I do this on my freshly swept garage floor, but you could also use a 4′ × 8′ sheet of plywood propped up on a table or sawhorses.

**1.** Tape the backing fabric right side down approximately every 10″ around the perimeter with masking tape.

**2.** *Lightly* spray the entire piece with basting spray, working on half of the fabric at a time. Hold a sheet of paper adjacent to the backing fabric to catch overspray.

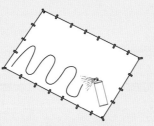

Spray half the fabric, then spray other half.

### Tip: Use "Just Enough" Spray

The most common mistake when using basting spray is using too much. Excess spray gums up machine needles and causes missed stitches. A light layer is all you need.

When spray basting for the first time, do a touch test on a small piece of fabric. After spraying, touch the fabric. It should stick to your finger when you pull away, but there shouldn't be any spray residue on your finger. If your finger feels tacky, you're spraying too much.

**3.** Gently press the batting onto the backing fabric, aligning all the edges as you press.

### Tip: Invite a Friend to Help

A second pair of hands makes spray basting much easier! One pair of hands holds two corners of the batting off of the tacky backing fabric while it is being pressed down nice and straight by the other pair of hands. If you can't line up an assistant, roll up the batting, set it on top of the sprayed backing fabric, and press the batting onto the backing as you unroll the batting, keeping all edges aligned.

### Pin Baste

For quilt-as-you-go projects, use straight pins if pin basting. They are quicker to remove than safety pins.

**1.** Tape the backing fabric right side down approximately every 10″ around the perimeter with masking tape.

**2.** Align the batting on top of the backing fabric.

**3.** Pin every 6″–8″. Place the pins parallel to the direction that you will roll the foundation when adding strips.

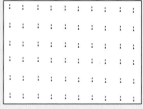

Foundation completely pin basted

**4.** Roll up the foundation to start sewing on strips.

Pins are parallel to the roll.

## Tiny Dresden Plates

*For detailed instructions refer to the Tiny and Mini Dresden Plate Assembly Techniques (page 16).*

**1.** Assemble Tiny Dresden plates using 12 Tiny Dresden petals from 2 charm squares, alternating the colors.

Make 25.

**2.** Appliqué a 1″ circle to the center of each of the 25 Tiny Dresden plates.

Make 25.

**3.** Remove the freezer paper templates, and then let the completed plates dry. Once dry, iron them with Best Press.

**Tip: Be Patient!**

**Let your plates dry. Pressing plates while they're still wet distorts them.**

**4.** Appliqué each Tiny Dresden plate to a charm square 5″ × 5″.

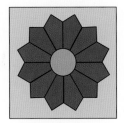

Make 25.

**5.** Sew together 5 Tiny Dresden blocks to make 1 row, pressing all the seams in the same direction.

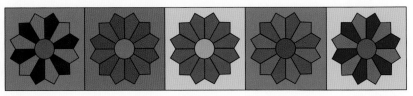

Make 5 rows.

## Sew the Rows to the Foundation

*Use a walking foot when sewing the rows to the foundation to ensure that all the layers stay together.*

**1.** Place the first Tiny Dresden block row *right side up* on the foundation, with the long edge even with the bottom edge of the foundation and the ends of the strip even with the sides of the foundation.

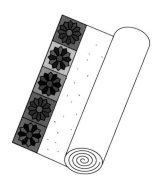

**2.** Place the second Tiny Dresden block row *right sides together* on top of the first Tiny Dresden block row, aligning all the edges.

**3.** Pin each seam allowance so that the seams are nesting, then pin again across the row pinning through both of the strips and the foundation.

**4.** With a walking foot, and with the foundation still rolled, sew a scant ¼″ seam allowance through all the layers. Set the stitch length to 7 stitches per inch. Remove pins as you sew if you pin basted.

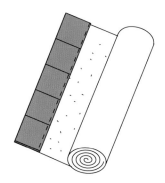

## Tip: Accuracy Counts

It's important to sew with an *exact* scant ¼" seam so you don't run out of foundation before completing the quilt. Sew on scraps of all the layers with your walking foot to find an accurate scant ¼" seam allowance.

**5.** Press the seam flat to set, and then press open.

**6.** Measure the quilt after sewing the strip onto the foundation to be sure you are sewing precisely. Even a small discrepancy can be a big problem when multiplied by the 5 strips on the quilt. For detailed instructions, refer to Press and Measure (below).

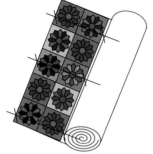

This measurement should be 9½" in all 3 places. Make necessary adjustments if it's not.

**7.** Repeat Steps 2–6 with the remaining 3 Tiny Dresden block rows. Measure after each addition, from the edge of the last strip back to the beginning edge of the quilt. After adding each row, the quilt should measure 14", 18½", and 23".

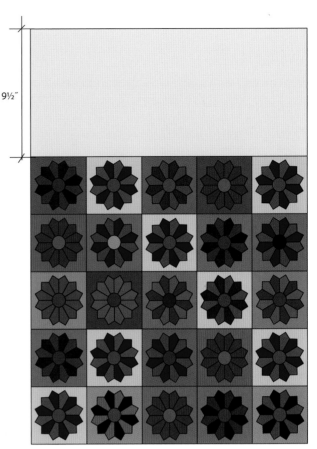

When all 5 rows have been added, there should be 9½" of foundation remaining.

# PRESS AND MEASURE

Pressing and measuring are key steps to keeping a quilt-as-you-go project straight. Follow these guidelines *after each strip is added* to your foundation.

**1.** Use a pressing surface big enough so that none of the quilt is hanging off an edge. (Sometimes 3 thick bath towels on a worktable is the way to go.)

**2.** Set the seam by first pressing it as it was sewn. Then open the strip and press again.

**3.** After each strip is pressed, measure from the edge of that strip back to the beginning edge of the quilt from both ends and from the center.

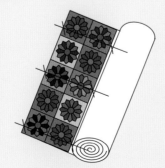

Measure from 3 locations.

**4.** If the measurement is the same in all 3 locations, add the next strip. If it's more than ⅛" off at any point, remove it and sew it on again. If the measurement is off by less than ⅛", make up the difference when you add the next strip. Place the new strip on top of the previously sewn strip with right sides together. The top strip will not align with the edge of the previous strip. It should be placed so the scant ¼" seam will correct the deficit of the previous strip. This may be accomplished by creating either a larger or smaller seam.

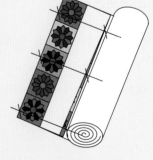

## Border

### APPLIQUÉ

*For more information, refer to the Quilt-as-You-Go Button Box appliqué pattern (the word "Quilts," pages 86 and 87).*

**1.** Trace the pattern onto the paper side of a piece of fusible web. (The pattern is already reversed for you.)

**2.** Fuse the traced letters onto the wrong side of the red letter fabric, following the manufacturer's instructions.

**3.** Cut out the letters on the drawn line.

**4.** Align the "Quilts" letters on the beige border rectangle 10″ × 23″.

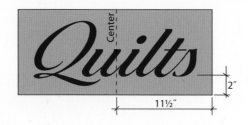

**5.** Fuse the letters in place.

**6.** Appliqué the letters to the border rectangle. (I used a button hole stitch on my machine with Sulky 12-weight Medium Taupe thread.)

**7.** Place the border strip on top of the last Tiny Dresden block row, with right sides together and all the edges aligned.

**8.** Pin the border strip in place and then sew it onto the quilt. Press.

**9.** The foundation should be perfectly filled.

## Finishing

**1.** Baste, then quilt the border. (I used a crosshatch pattern marked with a Chaco Liner every 2″ when machine quilting.)

**2.** Bind and label.

# Shimmering Dresdens

**Finished block:** 7½″ × 7½″
**Finished quilt:** 27″ × 27″

Changing the fabric in a block can change the entire look of a quilt. A stark contrast between the background fabric and the Tiny Dresden plates in these blocks make the Tiny Dresdens appear to be shimmering. In reality, it's the same block as in the quilt *All Roads Lead to Dresden* (page 80), but the look here is very different. When choosing fabrics for your quilts, keep in mind how contrast changes whether the Dresdens sit back or stand out.

Quilted by Tamara Lynn

## Materials

**Cream #1:** ⅓ yard for Tiny Dresden plate background

**Cream #2:** ⅔ yard for blocks

**Reds (3):** ⅓ yard of each red fabric for Tiny Dresden petals and blocks

**Green:** ¾ yard for sashing and binding

**Backing:** 1 yard

**Batting:** 35″ × 35″

**Freezer paper**

**Fabric glue:** Such as Roxanne Glue-Baste-It

**Thread:** To match fabrics

**That Purple Thang**

**Mary Ellen's Best Press:** In single-finger pump bottle

**Templates:** Suzn Quilts' Tiny Dresden Plate Template #216 (highly recommended)

**Paper cutter:** 1″ circle (recommended)

**Thangles:** For 1½″ finished half-square triangles (highly recommended)

## Cutting

*Before cutting, lightly spray each fabric with Mary Ellen's Best Press then iron dry as instructed in Best Press Dos and Don'ts (page 12). To cut petal shapes, use Suzn Quilts' Tiny Dresden Template #216 or the Tiny Dresden petal pattern (page 86). Please note the alternate cutting instructions if you are using Thangles to make half-square triangles.*

### Cream #1

• Cut 2 strips 5″ × width of fabric; subcut into 9 squares 5″ × 5″.

### Cream #2

• Cut 2 strips 2″ × width of fabric; subcut into 36 squares 2″ × 2″.

• Cut 4 strips 2½″ × width of fabric; subcut into 54 squares 2½″ × 2½″. *Or, if using Thangles,* cut 6 strips 2″ × width of fabric instead.

### Reds (3)

*From each red fabric:*

• Cut 2 strips 2″ × width of fabric; subcut into 36 Tiny Dresden Petals each (108 petals total).

• Cut 2 strips 2½″ × width of fabric each (6 strips total); subcut into 18 squares 2½″ × 2½″ each (54 squares total). *Or, if using Thangles,* cut 2 strips 2″ × width of fabric instead.

### Green

• Cut 5 strips 1½″ × width of fabric; subcut into 2 strips 1½″ × 27″, 4 strips 1½″ × 25″, and 6 strips 1½″ × 8″.

• Cut 3 strips 2½″ × width of fabric for binding.

### Freezer paper

• Cut 9 squares 1½″ × 1½″.

# Construction

*Seam allowances are scant ¼″ unless noted.*

## Make the Tiny Dresden Plates

*For detailed instructions, refer to Tiny and Mini Dresden Plate Assembly Techniques (page 16).*

**1.** Assemble 9 Tiny Dresden plates using the 108 red Tiny Dresden petals. Make each plate using 12 petals of the *same* red fabric.

Make 9.

**2.** Make 9 black 1″ centers and appliqué them to the Tiny Dresden plates.

Make 9.

**3.** Remove the freezer paper templates, and then let the completed plates dry. Once dry, iron them with Best Press.

### Tip: Be Patient!

**Let your plates dry. Pressing plates while they're still wet distorts them.**

**4.** Appliqué each Tiny Dresden plate to 1 cream square 5″ × 5″.

Make 9.

## Dresden Puzzle Blocks

*Unfinished block will measure 8″ × 8″.*

### HALF-SQUARE TRIANGLES

*If using Thangles, follow the manufacturer's instructions for 1½″ finished size and make 108 half-square triangles, skipping Steps 1–3.*

**1.** Place a cream square 2½″ × 2½″ on top of a red square 2½″ × 2½″ with right sides together.

**2.** Draw a diagonal line across a cream square. Stitch a scant ¼″ on both sides of that line.

**3.** Cut apart along the drawn line. Press the seams toward the red triangles. Trim each to a square 2″ × 2″.

Half-square triangle; make 108.

### ASSEMBLE THE BLOCKS

Sew together 12 half-square triangles, 4 cream squares 2″ × 2″, and 1 Tiny Dresden block as shown.

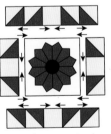

Press the seams in the direction of the arrows.

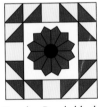

Dresden Puzzle block; make 9.

## Assemble the Quilt

**1.** Sew together 2 green sashing strips 1½″ × 8″ and 3 Dresden puzzle blocks as shown. Press the seams toward the sashing strips.

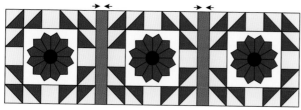

Make 3 rows.

**2.** Sew 2 green sashing strips 1½″ × 25″ between the rows. Press the seams toward the sashing strips.

**3.** Sew 2 green sashing strips 1½″ × 25″ onto the sides of the quilt and 2 green sashing strips 1½″ × 27″ onto the top and the bottom. Press the seams toward the green sashing strips.

*Shimmering Dresdens* quilt assembly

## Finishing

**1.** Layer the completed top with backing and batting.

**2.** Quilt, bind, and label.

# Dresden Ohio

**Finished block:** 4½″ × 4½″

**Finished quilt:** 41″ × 41″

Fabric placement is key in this quilt. I wanted the points of
the Ohio stars to be very evident so they are darker than the
rest of the block. Additionally, the dark centers of the Tiny Dresdens
add more drama while the alternate light squares show off the wonderful work
of my quilter, Tamara Lynn. The light squares would also make fun signature
blocks and you could easily add more rows to accommodate more signatures.

Quilted by Tamara Lynn

## Materials

**Cream:** 1 yard for Dresden block background and alternate blocks

**Gray:** ½ yard for Tiny Dresden petals

**Pink:** ¾ yard for hourglass blocks

**Purple:** ¾ yard for hourglass blocks

**Brown:** ¼ yard for Tiny Dresden centers

**Binding:** ½ yard

**Backing:** 2¾ yards

**Batting:** 49″ × 49″

**Freezer paper**

**Fabric glue:** Such as Roxanne Glue-Baste-It

**Thread:** To match fabrics

**That Purple Thang**

**Mary Ellen's Best Press:** In single-finger pump bottle

**Templates:** Suzn Quilts' Tiny Dresden Plate Template #216 (highly recommended)

**Paper cutter:** 1″ circle (highly recommended)

## Cutting

*Before cutting, lightly spray each fabric with Mary Ellen's Best Press then iron dry as instructed in Best Press Dos and Don'ts (page 12). To cut petal shapes, use Suzn Quilts' Tiny Dresden Template #216 or the Tiny Dresden petal pattern (page 86).*

### Cream

- Cut 6 strips 5″ × width of fabric; subcut into 41 squares 5″ × 5″.

### Pink

- Cut 4 strips 7″ × width of fabric; subcut into 20 squares 7″ × 7″.

### Purple

- Cut 4 strips 7″ × width of fabric; subcut into 20 squares 7″ × 7″.

### Gray

- Cut 6 strips 2″ × width of fabric; subcut into 192 Tiny Dresden petals.

### Binding

- Cut 5 strips 2½″ × width of fabric.

### Freezer paper

- Cut 16 squares 1½″ × 1½″.

# Construction

*Seam allowances are scant ¼″ unless noted.*

## Tiny Dresden Plates

*For detailed instructions, refer to Tiny and Mini Dresden Plate Assembly Techniques (page 16).*

**1.** Assemble 16 Tiny Dresden plates using the 192 Tiny Dresden petals.

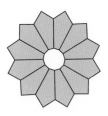

**2.** Make 16 brown 1″ centers and appliqué them to the Tiny Dresden plates.

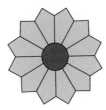

**3.** Remove the freezer paper templates then let the completed plates dry. Once dry, iron them with Best Press.

**Tip: Be Patient!**

Let your plates dry. Pressing plates while they're still wet distorts them.

**4.** Appliqué each of the 16 Tiny Dresden plates to 1 cream background square 5″ × 5″.

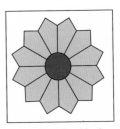

Tiny Dresden block; make 16.

## Hourglass Blocks

**1.** Place a pink square 7″ × 7″ on top of a purple square 7″ × 7″ with right sides together.

**2.** Draw a diagonal line across the pink square. Stitch a scant ¼″ on both sides of that line.

**3.** Cut apart along the drawn line.

**4.** Press the seam flat to set, and then press toward the purple triangle.

Half-square triangle; make 40.

**5.** Draw a line perpendicular to the sewn seam on the wrong side of 1 half-square triangle. Place it on top of another half-square triangle, with right sides together, purple on top, pin so the seam allowances nest. Pin in place, and sew a scant ¼″ on both sides of the drawn line.

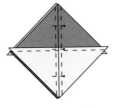

**6.** Cut apart the unit on the drawn line. Press the seams to set, and then press to one side. Trim to 5″ × 5″.

Hourglass block; make 40.

# Assemble the Quilt

**1.** Sew together 4 hourglass blocks and 5 cream background squares 5″ × 5″ as shown. Press the seams toward the cream background squares.

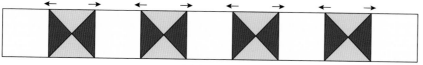

Make 5.

**2.** Sew together 5 hourglass blocks and 4 Tiny Dresden Blocks. Press the seams toward the cream background squares.

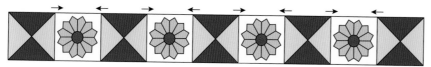

Make 4.

**3.** Sew together the rows to complete the quilt as shown.

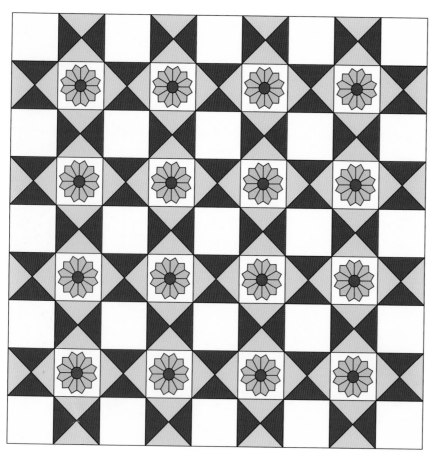

*Dresden Ohio* quilt assembly

# Finishing

**1.** Layer the completed top with backing and batting.

**2.** Quilt, bind, and label.

# Follow Me

This simple design is oh so cute!

**Finished blocks:** 4½″ × 4½″ and 9″ × 9″

**Finished quilt:** 42½″ × 42½″

Quilted by Tamara Lynn

## Materials

**Pink/cream print:** 1 yard for Dresden plate background

**Pink #1:** ½ yard for Dresden petals

**Pink #2:** ½ yard for Dresden petals

**Cream:** ¾ yard for Flying Geese

**Green #1:** ⅓ yard for Flying Geese

**Green #2:** ⅔ yard for Flying Geese and binding

**Green #3:** ½ yard for border

**Black:** ¼ yard for Dresden plate centers

**Backing:** 3 yards

**Batting:** 50½″ × 50½″

**Freezer paper**

**Fabric glue:** Such as Roxanne Glue-Baste-It

**Thread:** To match fabrics

**That Purple Thang**

**Mary Ellen's Best Press:** In single-finger pump bottle

**Templates:**

• Suzn Quilts' Tiny Dresden Plate Template #216 (highly recommended)

• Suzn Quilts' Mini Dresden Plate Template #186 (highly recommended)

**Paper cutters:**

• 1″ circle (recommended)

• 2″ circle (recommended)

## Cutting

*Before cutting, lightly spray each fabric with Mary Ellen's Best Press then iron dry as instructed in Best Press Dos and Don'ts (page 12). To cut petal shapes, use Suzn Quilts' Tiny Dresden Template #216 and Mini Dresden Template #186 or the Tiny and Mini Dresden petal patterns (page 86).*

### Pink/cream print

• Cut 3 strips 9½″ × width of fabric; subcut into 9 squares 9½″ × 9½″. Trim the remainder of the strip to 5″; subcut into 4 squares 5″ × 5″.

### Pink #1

• Cut 3 strips 3½″ × width of fabric; subcut strips into 54 Mini Dresden petals (54 total).

• Cut 1 strip 2″ × width of fabric; subcut strips into 24 Tiny Dresden petals.

### Pink #2

• Cut 3 strips 3½″ × width of fabric; subcut strips into 54 Mini Dresden petals (54 total).

• Cut 1 strip 2″ × width of fabric; subcut strips into 24 Tiny Dresden petals.

### Cream

• Cut 7 strips 2¾″ × width of fabric; subcut into 96 squares 2¾″ × 2¾″.

### Green #1

• Cut 3 strips 2¾″ × width of fabric; subcut into 24 rectangles 2¾″ × 5″.

### Green #2

• Cut 3 strips 2¾″ × width of fabric; subcut into 24 rectangles 2¾″ × 5″.

• Cut 5 strips 2½″ × width of fabric for binding.

### Green #3

• Cut 4 strips 3½″ × width of fabric; subcut into 2 strips 3½″ × 36½″ and 2 strips 3½″ × 42½″.

### Freezer paper

• Cut 9 squares 2½″ × 2½″.

• Cut 4 squares 1½″ × 1½″.

# Construction

*Seam allowances are scant ¼″ unless noted.*

## Make the Mini Dresden and Tiny Dresden Plates

*For detailed instructions, refer to Tiny and Mini Dresden Plate Assembly Techniques (page 16).*

**1.** Assemble 9 Mini Dresden plates using the 108 Mini Dresden petals and alternating the 2 pink fabrics.

**2.** Assemble 4 Tiny Dresden plates using the 48 Tiny Dresden petals and alternating the 2 pink fabrics.

**3.** Make 9 black 2″ centers and appliqué them to the Mini Dresden plates.

**4.** Make 4 black 1″ centers and appliqué them to the Tiny Dresden plates.

Make 9.

Make 4.

Make 9.

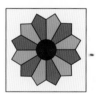

Make 4.

**5.** Remove the freezer paper templates, and then let the completed plates dry. Once dry, iron them with Best Press.

### Tip: Be Patient!

Let your plates dry. Pressing plates while they're still wet distorts them.

**6.** Appliqué the Mini Dresden plates to the pink/cream squares 9½″ × 9½″.

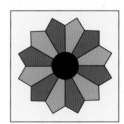

Make 9.

**7.** Appliqué the Tiny Dresden plates to the cream/pink squares 5″ × 5″.

Make 4.

## Flying Geese Blocks

**1.** Place a cream square 2¾″ × 2¾″ on top of a green rectangle 2¾″ × 5″, with right sides together.

**2.** Draw a diagonal line across the cream square. Stitch on that line. Trim away both fabrics ¼″ outside that line. Press the seam to set, and then press toward the cream fabric.

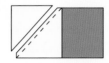

**3.** Repeat Steps 1 and 2 using another cream square 2¾″ × 2¾″ on the opposite corner. Trim then press.

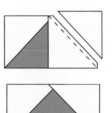

Make 48.

**4.** Sew together 4 Flying Geese as shown. Press the seams toward the green fabric.

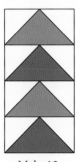

Make 12.

## Assemble the Quilt

**1.** Sew 1 Mini Dresden plate block together with 1 Flying Geese block. Note the direction of the Flying Geese. Press the seam toward the Dresden plate block.

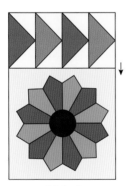

Make 2.

**2.** Sew 1 Mini Dresden plate block together with 1 Flying Geese block, reversing the direction of the Flying Geese. Press the seam toward the Mini Dresden plate block.

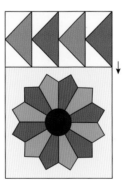

Make 6.

**3.** Sew 1 Tiny Dresden plate block together with 1 Flying Geese block. Note the direction of the Flying Geese. Press the seams toward the Tiny Dresden plate block.

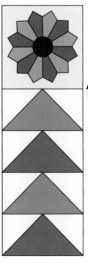

Make 4.

**4.** Sew the blocks into rows and press.

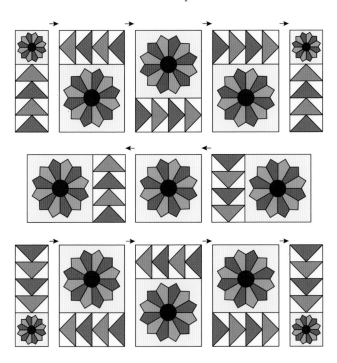

**5.** Sew together the 3 rows and press the seams in direction of arrows.

**6.** Sew the 2 green border strips 3½″ × 36½″ to the sides of the quilt. Press the seams toward the borders.

**7.** Sew the green border strips 3½″ × 42½″ to the top and bottom of the quilt. Press the seams toward the borders.

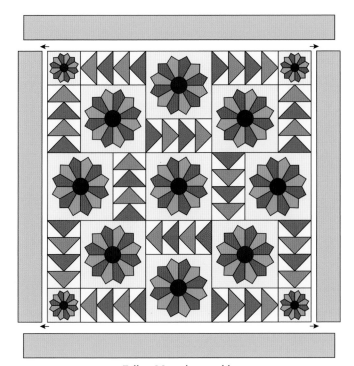

*Follow Me* quilt assembly

# Finishing

**1.** Layer the completed top with backing and batting.

**2.** Quilt, bind, and label.

# Spring Fair

**Finished blocks:** 4½″ × 4½″ and 9″ × 9″
**Finished quilt:** 36½″ × 36½″

The way the Tiny Dresden plates surround the center Mini Dresden plate in this quilt reminds me of a Ferris Wheel at a spring fair. My favorite Dresden plates feature two fabrics for the petals, and here the alternating colors just add to the fun.

Quilted by Tamara Lynn

## Materials

**Cream:** 1 yard for background

**Light gray:** ½ yard for center block background and outer corner block background

**Pink #1:** ⅓ yard for Dresden petals

**Pink #2:** ⅓ yard for Dresden petals

**Medium gray:** ½ yard center star points, Churn Dash corners, and outer border

**Gold:** ⅓ yard for Churn Dash blocks

**Charcoal:** ½ yard for Churn Dash blocks and binding

**Backing:** 1¼ yards

**Batting:** 44½″ × 44½″

**Freezer paper**

**Fabric glue:** Such as Roxanne Glue-Baste-It

**Thread:** To match fabrics

**That Purple Thang**

**Mary Ellen's Best Press:** In single-finger pump bottle

**Templates:**

- Suzn Quilts' Tiny Dresden Plate Template #216 (highly recommended)

- Suzn Quilts' Mini Dresden Plate Template #186 (highly recommended)

**Paper cutters:**

- 1″ circle (recommended)

- 2″ circle (recommended)

## Cutting

*Before cutting, lightly spray each fabric with Mary Ellen's Best Press then iron dry as instructed in Best Press Dos and Don'ts (page 12). To cut petal shapes, use Suzn Quilts' Tiny Dresden Template #216 and Mini Dresden Template #186 or the Tiny and Mini Dresden petal patterns (page 86).*

### Cream

- Cut 6 strips 5″ × width of fabric; subcut into 4 strips 4″ × 27½″, 4 rectangles 5″ × 9½″, and 12 squares 5″ × 5″.

### Light gray

- Cut 1 strip 9½″; subcut 1 square 9½″ × 9½″. Trim remainder of strip to 5″; subcut into 4 squares 5″ × 5″.

### Pink #1

- Cut 1 strip 3½″ × width of fabric; subcut into 6 Mini Dresden petals.

- Cut 3 strips 2″ × width of fabric; subcut into 96 Tiny Dresden petals.

### Pink #2

- Cut 1 strip 3½″ × width of fabric; subcut into 6 Mini Dresden petals.

- Cut 3 strips 2″ × width of fabric; subcut into 96 Tiny Dresden petals.

### Medium gray

- Cut 1 strip 5″ × width of fabric; subcut into 8 squares 5″ × 5″.

- Cut 4 strips 1½″ × width of fabric; subcut into 4 strips 1½″ × 27½″.

- Cut 1 strip 3¼″ × width of fabric; subcut into 8 squares 3¼″ × 3¼″.

### Gold

- Cut 2 strips 1¾″ × width of fabric.

- Cut 1 strip 3¼″ × width of fabric; subcut into 8 squares 3¼″ × 3¼″.

### Charcoal

- Cut 2 strips 1½″ × width of fabric.

- Cut 4 strips 2½″ × width of fabric for binding.

### Freezer paper

- Cut 1 square 2½″ × 2½″.

- Cut 16 squares 1½″ × 1½″.

# Construction

*Seam allowances are scant ¼" unless noted.*

## Mini Dresden and Tiny Dresden Plates

*For detailed instructions, refer to Tiny and Mini Dresden Plate Assembly Techniques (page 16).*

**1.** Assemble 1 Mini Dresden plate using the 12 Mini Dresden petals and alternating the 2 pink fabrics.

Make 1.

**2.** Assemble 16 Tiny Dresden plates using the 192 Tiny Dresden petals and alternating the 2 pink fabrics.

Make 16.

**3.** Make 1 charcoal 2" center and appliqué it to the Mini Dresden plate.

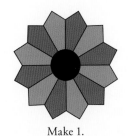

Make 1.

**4.** Make 16 pink 1" centers and appliqué them to the Tiny Dresden plates.

Make 16.

**5.** Remove the freezer paper templates, and then let the completed plates dry. Once dry, iron them with Best Press.

**Tip: Be Patient!**

Let your plates dry. Pressing plates while they're still wet distorts them.

**6.** Appliqué the Mini Dresden plate to the light gray background square 9½" × 9½".

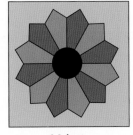

Make 1.

**7.** Appliqué 12 Tiny Dresden plates to the cream background square 5" × 5" and appliqué 4 Tiny Dresden plates to a light gray background square 5" × 5".

Make 12.

Make 4.

## Churn Dash Blocks

*Unfinished block measures 9½" × 9½".*

### STRIP SETS

**1.** Sew 1 gold strip 1¾" to 1 charcoal strip 1½" along the long edge, with right sides together. Press the seam to set, and then press toward the charcoal fabric. Repeat to make 2.

**2.** Cut each strip set into 8 rectangles 2¾" × 5".

Make 16.

### HALF-SQUARE TRIANGLES

**1.** Place a gold square 3¼" × 3¼" on top of a medium gray square 3¼" × 3¼", with right sides together.

**2.** Draw a diagonal line across the gold square. Stitch a scant ¼" on both sides of that line.

**3.** Cut apart along drawn line. Press the seams toward the medium gray triangles. Trim each to a 2¾" × 2¾" square.

Make 16.

## ASSEMBLE THE BLOCKS

Sew together a cream background Tiny Dresden block, 4 half-square triangles, and 4 strip sets to make a Churn Dash block.

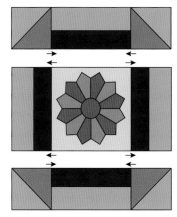

Churn Dash block; make 4.
Press seams in direction of arrows.

# Flying Geese

**1.** Place a medium gray square 5″ × 5″ on top of a cream rectangle 5″ × 9½″, with right sides together.

**2.** Draw a diagonal line across the gray square. Stitch on that line. Trim away both fabrics ¼″ outside the line. Press the seam to set, then press toward the medium gray fabric.

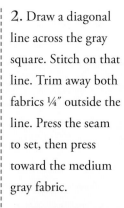

**3.** Repeat using another medium gray square 5″ × 5″ on the opposite corner. Trim then press.

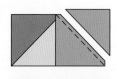

Flying Geese; make 4.

# Alternate Blocks

Sew together 2 cream background Tiny Dresden blocks side by side and press. Sew a Flying Geese to these 2 blocks and press.

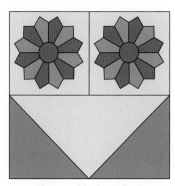

Alternate block; make 4.

# Assemble the Border

**1.** Sew together each medium gray strip 1½″ × 27½″ with a cream strip 4″ × 27½″, right sides together. Press the seam to set, then toward the medium gray fabric.

Make 4.

**2.** Sew 2 Tiny Dresden blocks onto each end of a medium gray/cream strip set. Press the seams toward the strip set.

Make 2.

## Assemble the Quilt

**1.** Sew the blocks into 3 rows, pressing the seams as indicated by the arrows.

**2.** Sew together the 3 rows and press the seams as you like.

**3.** Sew the side borders onto the quilt, and then add the top and bottom borders. Press the seams as indicated.

*Spring Fair* quilt assembly

## Finishing

**1.** Layer the completed top with backing and batting.

**2.** Quilt, bind, and label.

# Friendship Garden

**Finished blocks:** 4½″ × 4½″ and 9″ × 9″
**Finished quilt:** 42½″ × 42½″

Did I tell you that I only quilt because I love fabric? OK, that's not the *only* reason, but it's a big factor. My favorite part of the process is putting together fabrics and the more of them that I can successfully squeeze into a single quilt, the happier I am. I used two purple fabrics and two black fabrics in this quilt, but one of each would be plenty. Did I mention that I love fabric?

Quilted by Tamara Lynn

## Materials

**Cream:** ⅔ yard for Dresden petals

**White:** ¼ yard for lining Dresden petals (only necessary if using a light Dresden petal fabric with a dark background, as shown in this quilt.)

**Beige:** ⅞ yard for Churn Dash blocks and outer border

**Purple #1:** 1¼ yards for Churn Dash blocks and inner border

**Purple #2:** ¼ yard for Dresden plate centers

**Black #1:** ¾ yard for Dresden plate background

**Black #2:** ⅝ yard for inner border and binding

**Backing:** 3 yards

**Batting:** 50½″ × 50½″

**Freezer paper**

**Fabric glue:** Such as Roxanne Glue-Baste-It

**Thread:** To match fabrics

**That Purple Thang**

**Mary Ellen's Best Press:** In single-finger pump bottle

**Templates:**

• Suzn Quilts' Tiny Dresden Plate Template #216 (highly recommended)

• Suzn Quilts' Mini Dresden Plate Template #186 (highly recommended)

**Paper cutters:**

• 1″ circle (recommended)

• 2″ circle (recommended)

## Cutting

*Before cutting, lightly spray each fabric with Mary Ellen's Best Press then iron dry as instructed in Best Press Dos and Don'ts (page 12). To cut petal shapes, use Suzn Quilts' Tiny Dresden Template #216 and Mini Dresden Template #186 or the Tiny and Mini Dresden petal patterns (page 86).*

### Cream

• Cut 2 strips 3½″ × width of fabric; subcut into 48 Mini Dresden petals.

• Cut 4 strips 2″ × width of fabric; subcut into 108 Tiny Dresden petals.

### Beige

• Cut 3 strips 1¾″ × width of fabric.

• Cut 5 strips 2¾″ × width of fabric; subcut into 4 strips 2¾″ × 28½″, 8 rectangles 2¾″ × 5″, and 4 squares 2¾″ × 2¾″.

• Cut 1 strip 3¼″ × width of fabric; subcut into 10 squares 3¼″ × 3¼″.

### Purple

• Cut 3 strips 1½″ × width of fabric.

• Cut 4 strips 5″ × width of fabric; subcut into 4 strips 5″ × 28½″.

• Cut 1 strips 3¼″ × width of fabric; subcut into 10 squares 3¼″ × 3¼″.

• Cut 2 strips 2¾″ × width of fabric; subcut into 16 squares 2¾″ × 2¾″.

### Black #1

• Cut 1 strip 9½″ × width of fabric; subcut into 4 squares 9½″ × 9½″.

• Cut 2 strips 5″ × width of fabric; subcut into 9 squares 5″ × 5″.

### Black #2

• Cut 4 strips 1″ × width of fabric; subcut into 2 strips 1″ × 27½″ and 2 strips 1″ × 28½″.

• Cut 5 strips 2½″ × width of fabric for binding.

### Freezer paper

• Cut 4 squares 2½″ × 2½″.

• Cut 9 squares 1½″ × 1½″.

# Construction

*Seam allowances are scant ¼″ unless noted.*

## Mini Dresden and Tiny Dresden Plates

*For detailed instructions, refer to Tiny and Mini Dresden Plate Assembly Techniques (pages 16).*

### ASSEMBLE PLATES

**1.** Assemble Mini Dresden plates using the 48 cream Mini Dresden petals.

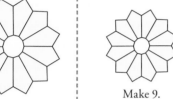

Make 4.

**2.** Assemble Tiny Dresden plates using the 108 cream Tiny Dresden petals.

Make 9.

### DRESDEN LINING

*Optional: If the fabric used for the Dresden plates is so light that the background fabric shows through, line the plates with white fabric as instructed.*

**1.** Cut 9 white 2¾″ circles for the Tiny Dresden plate liners.

**2.** Cut 4 white 5″ circles for the Mini Dresden plate liners.

**3.** Glue the circle of white fabric to the back of each Dresden plate. When the Dresden center is appliquéd to the plate it will hold the lining in place.

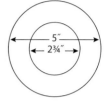

### FINISH PLATES

**1.** Use purple #2 to make 4 centers 2″ and appliqué them to the Mini Dresden plates.

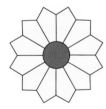

**2.** Use purple #2 to make 9 centers 1″ and appliqué them to the Tiny Dresden plates.

**3.** Remove the freezer paper templates, and then let the completed plates dry. Note, if you've lined the plates, you will need to carefully cut a slit through the lining circles to remove the paper templates. Once dry, iron them with Best Press.

### Tip: Be Patient!

**Let your plates dry. Pressing plates while they're still wet distorts them.**

**4.** Appliqué the Mini Dresden plates to the black squares 9½″ × 9½″.

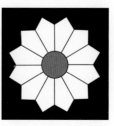

Make 4.

**5.** Appliqué the Tiny Dresden plates to the black squares 5″ × 5″.

Make 9.

# Dresden Churn Dash Blocks

*Unfinished blocks will measure 9½" × 9½".*

### STRIP SETS

1. Sew together a beige strip 1¾" and a purple strip 1½" along one long edge, with right sides together. Press flat to set, and then press toward the purple fabric. Make three strip sets.

2. Cut 20 rectangles 2¾" × 5" from the strips.

Cut 20.

### HALF-SQUARE TRIANGLES

1. Place a beige square 3¼" × 3¼" on top of a purple square 3¼" × 3¼", with right sides together.

2. Draw a diagonal line across the beige square. Stitch a scant ¼" on both sides of that line.

3. Cut apart along the drawn line. Press the seams toward the purple triangles. Trim each to 2¾" × 2¾" square.

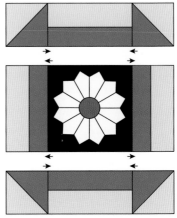

Make 20.

### ASSEMBLE THE BLOCKS

Sew together a Tiny Dresden block, 4 half-square triangles, and 4 strip sets as shown.

Churn Dash block; make 5.
Press in the direction of the arrows.

# Assemble the Quilt

1. Sew the Dresden Churn Dash blocks and the Mini Dresden plate blocks into rows as shown. Press the seams toward the Mini Dresden plate blocks. Sew together the rows. Press the seams as you like.

2. Sew black strips 1" × 27½" onto the sides of the quilt then sew the black strips 1" × 28½" onto the top and bottom of the quilt. Press the seams toward the black strips.

## Flying Geese Blocks

**1.** Place a purple square 2¾" × 2¾" on top of a beige rectangle 2¾" × 5", with right sides together.

**2.** Draw a diagonal line across the purple square. Stitch on that line. Trim away both fabrics ¼" outside that line. Press the seam flat to set, and then press toward the purple fabric.

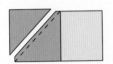

**3.** Repeat using another purple square 2¾" × 2¾" on the opposite corner. Trim then press.

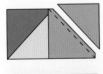

Make 8.

## Assemble the Border

**1.** Sew together a beige strip 2¾" × 28½" and a purple strip 5" × 28½" along one long edge, with right sides together. Press the seam flat to set, and then press toward the purple fabric.

Make 4.

**2.** Sew together 2 Flying Geese blocks with a Tiny Dresden block and a beige 2¾" × 2¾" square to make a corner block. Press the seams away from the Flying Geese blocks.

**3.** Sew 2 corner blocks onto a beige/purple strip set. Press the seams toward the strip sets.

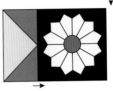

Corner block; make 4

Make 2.

**4.** Sew 2 remaining beige/purple strip sets to the sides of the quilt, then sew the strip sets with corner blocks onto the top and bottom of the quilt. Press the seams away from the black strips.

*Friendship Garden* quilt assembly

## Finishing

**1.** Layer the completed top with backing and batting.

**2.** Quilt, bind, and label.

# All Roads Lead to Dresden

**Finished blocks:** 4½″ × 4½″ and 7½″ × 7½″

**Finished quilt:** 33½″ × 33½″

I love dropping a little Dresden plate into a traditional or traditional-ish block. Designing this quilt was easy—the hard part was deciding where to place fabrics so that the pattern turned out just right. With only a few colors, the juxtaposition of blocks makes for a lot of movement in this big-impact quilt.

Quilted by Tamara Lynn

## Materials

**Cream:** ½ yard for Dresden puzzle blocks

**Beige:** ½ yard for Dresden plate background and Flying Geese blocks

**Light gold:** ¾ yard for Tiny and Mini Dresden petals and Dresden puzzle blocks

**Dark gold:** ¾ yard for Tiny Dresden and Mini Dresden petals and star points

**Blue #1:** ¼ yard for Tiny Dresden petals

**Blue #2:** ½ yard for corner squares, Tiny Dresden centers, and star background

**Black:** ⅝ yard for Flying Geese blocks, Dresden centers and binding

**Backing:** 1¼ yards

**Batting:** 41″ × 41″

**Freezer paper**

**Fabric glue:** Such as Roxanne Glue-Baste-It

**Thread:** To match fabrics

**That Purple Thang**

**Mary Ellen's Best Press:** In single-finger pump bottle

**Thangles:** For half-square triangle 1½″ (recommended)

**Templates:**

- Suzn Quilts' Tiny Dresden Plate Template #216 (highly recommended)

- Suzn Quilts' Mini Dresden Plate Template #186 (highly recommended)

**Paper cutters:**

- 1″ circle (recommended)

- 2″ circle (recommended)

## Cutting

*Before cutting, lightly spray each fabric with Mary Ellen's Best Press, then iron dry as instructed in Best Press Dos and Don'ts (page 12). To cut petal shapes, use Suzn Quilts' Tiny Dresden Template #216 and Mini Dresden Template #186 or the Tiny and Mini Dresden petal patterns (page 86). Please note the alternate cutting instructions if you are using Thangles to make half-square triangles.*

### Cream

- Cut 2 strips 2″ × width of fabric; subcut into 32 squares 2″ × 2″.

- Cut 4 strips 2½″ × width of fabric; subcut into 48 squares 2½″ × 2½″. *Or, if using Thangles, cut 4 strips 2″ × width of fabric instead.*

### Beige

- Cut 1 strip 9½″ × width of fabric; subcut into 1 square 9½″ × 9½″ and 4 squares 5″ × 5″.

- Cut 2 strips 2″ × width of fabric; subcut into 56 squares 2″ × 2″.

### Light gold

- Cut 1 strip 5″ × width of fabric; subcut into 8 squares 5″ × 5″.

- Cut 1 strip 3½″ × width of fabric; subcut into 6 Mini Dresden petals.

- Cut 1 strip 2″ × width of fabric; subcut into 24 Tiny Dresden petals.

- Cut 4 strips 2½″ × width of fabric; subcut into 48 squares 2½″ × 2½″. *Or, if using Thangles, cut 4 strips 2″ × width of fabric instead.*

### Dark gold

- Cut 1 strip 3½″ × width of fabric; subcut into 8 rectangles 3½″ × 5″.

- Cut 1 strip 2″ × width of fabric; subcut into 8 squares 2″ × 2″.

- Cut 1 strip 3½″ × width of fabric; subcut into 6 Mini Dresden petals.

- Cut 3 strips 2″ × width of fabric; subcut into 96 Tiny Dresden petals.

### Blue #1

- Cut 1 strip 2″ × width of fabric. Cut 24 Tiny Dresden petals.

### Blue #2

- Cut 1 strip 9½″ × width of fabric; subcut into 4 squares 9½″ × 9½″.

- Cut 1 strip 3½″ × width of fabric; subcut into 8 squares 3½″ × 3½″.

### Black

- Cut 2 strips 3½″ × width of fabric; subcut into 32 rectangles 2″ × 3½″.

- Cut 4 strips 2½″ for binding.

### Freezer paper

- Cut 1 square 2½″ × 2½″.

- Cut 12 squares 1½″ × 1½″.

# Construction

*Seam allowances are scant ¼″ unless noted.*

## Mini Dresden and Tiny Dresden Plates

*For detailed instructions, refer to Tiny and Mini Dresden Plate Assembly Techniques (page 16).*

**1.** Assemble 1 Mini Dresden plate alternating the 6 light gold and 6 dark gold Mini Dresden petals.

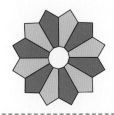

**2.** Assemble 8 Tiny Dresden plates using the 96 dark gold Tiny Dresden petals.

Make 8.

**3.** Assemble 4 Tiny Dresden plates alternating the 24 light gold and 24 blue #1 Tiny Dresden petals.

Make 4.

**4.** Make 1 black 2″ center and appliqué it to the Mini Dresden plate.

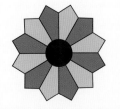

**5.** Make 8 black 1″ centers and appliqué them to the dark gold Tiny Dresden plates.

Make 8.

**6.** Make 4 blue #2 centers 1″ and appliqué them to the blue/gold Tiny Dresden plates.

Make 4.

**7.** Remove the freezer paper templates, and then let the completed plates dry. Once dry, iron them with Best Press.

### Tip: Be Patient!

**Let your plates dry. Pressing plates while they're still wet distorts them.**

**8.** Appliqué the gold Mini Dresden plate to the beige square 9½″ × 9½″.

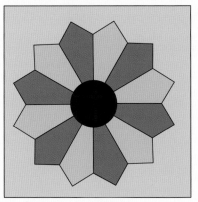

Make 1.

**9.** Appliqué the 8 dark gold Tiny Dresden plates to the 8 light gold squares 5″ × 5″.

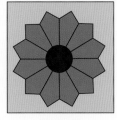

Make 8.

**10.** Appliqué the 4 light gold/blue #1 Tiny Dresden plates to the 4 beige squares 5″ × 5″.

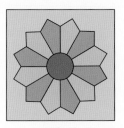

Make 4.

# Dresden Puzzle Blocks

## HALF-SQUARE TRIANGLES

*If using Thangles, follow the manufacturer's instructions for 1½" finished size and make 96 half-square triangles, skipping Steps 1–3.*

**1.** Place a cream square 2½" × 2½" on top of a light gold square 2½" × 2½", with right sides together.

**2.** Draw a diagonal line across the cream square. Stitch a scant ¼" on both sides of that line.

**3.** Cut apart along drawn line. Press to set, then press toward the light gold triangle. Trim each to a 2" × 2" square.

Make 96.

## ASSEMBLE THE BLOCKS

**1.** Sew together 12 half-square triangles, 4 cream squares 2" × 2", and a dark gold Tiny Dresden plate block as shown.

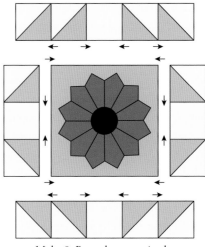

Make 8. Press the seams in the direction of the arrows.

# Flying Geese

**1.** Place a beige square 2" × 2" on top of a black rectangle 2" × 3½", with right sides together.

**2.** Draw a diagonal line across the beige square. Stitch on that line. Trim away both fabrics ¼" outside the line. Press the seam flat to set, and then press toward the beige fabric.

**3.** Repeat Steps 1 and 2 using another beige square 2" × 2" on the opposite corner. Trim, then press.

Flying Geese; make 28.

**4.** Repeat Steps 1–3 to make 4 more Flying Geese using the remaining 4 black rectangles 2" × 3½" and 8 dark gold squares 2" × 2".

Flying Geese; make 4.

## Half–Flying Geese

**1.** Place a blue #2 square 3½" × 3½" on top of a dark gold rectangle 3½" × 5", with right sides together and the left edges aligned.

**2.** Draw a diagonal line across the blue #2 square as shown. Stitch on that line. Trim away both fabrics ¼" outside that line.

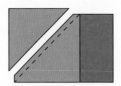

**3.** Press the seam flat to set, and then press toward the blue #2 fabric.

Half Flying Geese; make 4. Note the orientation of the blue triangle.

**4.** Place a blue #2 square 3½" × 3½" on top of *opposite* corner of another dark gold rectangle 3½" × 5", with right sides together and the right edges aligned.

**5.** Draw a diagonal line across the blue #2 square as shown. Stitch on that line. Trim away both fabrics ¼" outside that line.

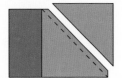

**6.** Press the seam flat as sewn, and then press the seam toward the blue #2 fabric.

Half–Flying Geese; make 4. Note the orientation of the blue triangle.

## Assemble the Quilt

**1.** Sew together 5 black/beige Flying Geese blocks. Press the seams toward the black fabric.

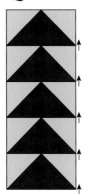

Make 4.

**2.** Sew together 2 black/beige Flying Geese blocks and 1 black/dark gold Flying Geese block. Press the seams toward the black fabric.

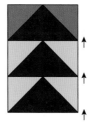

Make 4.

**3.** Sew together 1 block of 5 Flying Geese and 2 Dresden puzzle blocks. Press open the seams.

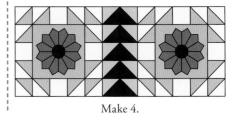

Make 4.

**4.** Sew together 1 block of 3 Flying Geese and 2 half Flying Geese blocks. Press the seams toward the half Flying Geese blocks.

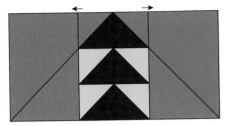

Make 4.

**5.** Sew together 2 blue/gold Tiny Dresden blocks and 1 Flying Geese unit. Press the seams toward the Tiny Dresden blocks.

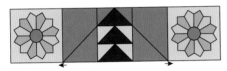

Make 2.

**6.** Sew together the Mini Dresden plate with the 2 remaining units.

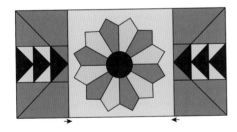

**7.** Sew together the 3 center rows. Press the seams toward the center.

**8.** Sew together all the units into 3 rows, and then sew together the rows to finish the quilt. Press the seams open.

### Tip

**When so many seams come together, it's easiest to press them open.**

*All Roads Lead to Dresden* quilt assembly

## Finishing

**1.** Layer the completed top with backing and batting.

**2.** Quilt, bind, and label.

# Patterns

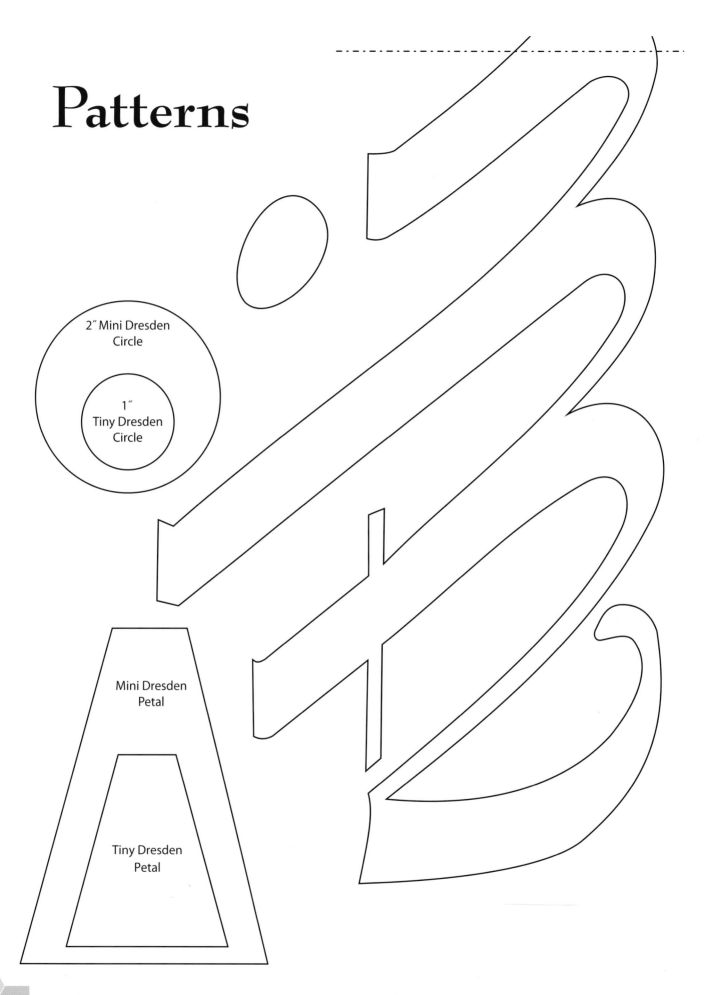

2″ Mini Dresden Circle

1″ Tiny Dresden Circle

Mini Dresden Petal

Tiny Dresden Petal

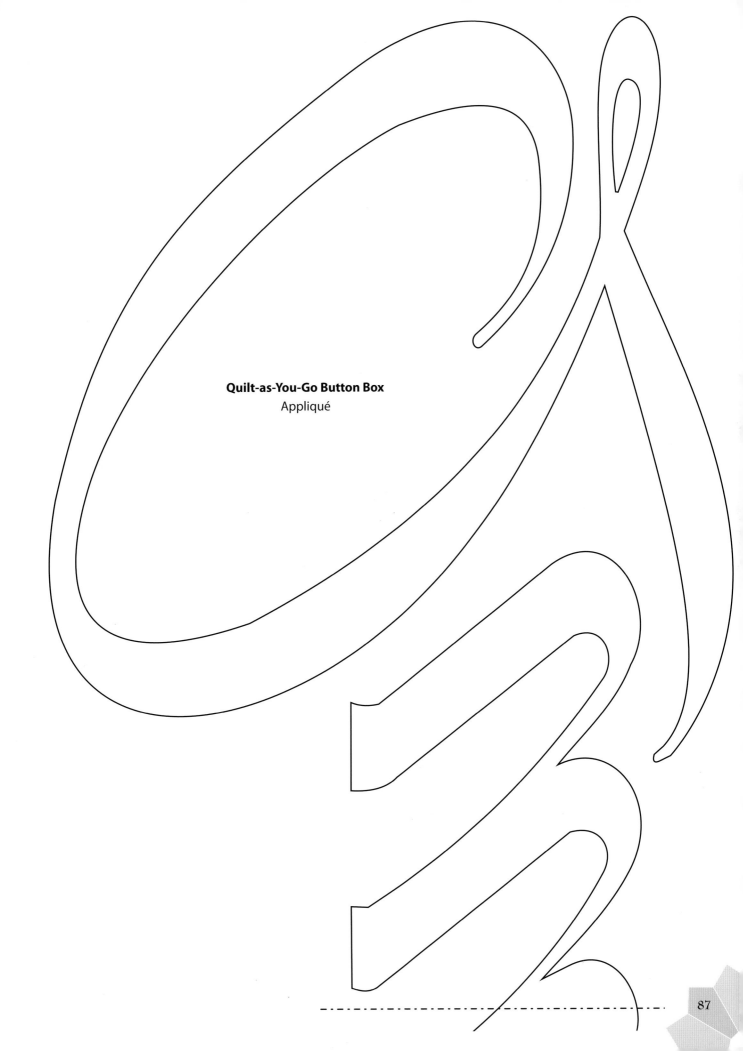

**Quilt-as-You-Go Button Box**
Appliqué

# About the Author

As early as second grade, Susan's designing ability was evident to her classmates as they crowded around her desk during rainy day recesses waiting in line for her to draw doodles for them to color. Years later, with a bachelor's degree in architectural interior design, she drafted office designs for clients in major corporate buildings in the St. Louis, Missouri, metropolitan area.

Today, Susan designs for her business, Suzn Quilts, using the same skills she began honing at an early age. In addition to creating hundreds of patterns and writing books, Susan also designs quilting fabric and quilts for magazines. She attends International Quilt Market twice annually selling to the trade. Her quilt patterns, books, and templates are sold internationally through quilt shops, catalogs, and distributors.

Susan enjoys lecturing, teaching workshops, and sharing her joy of quilting and design with others. For information about Susan's patterns, books, and templates, or her teaching availability, please visit suznquilts.com.

Susan R. Marth

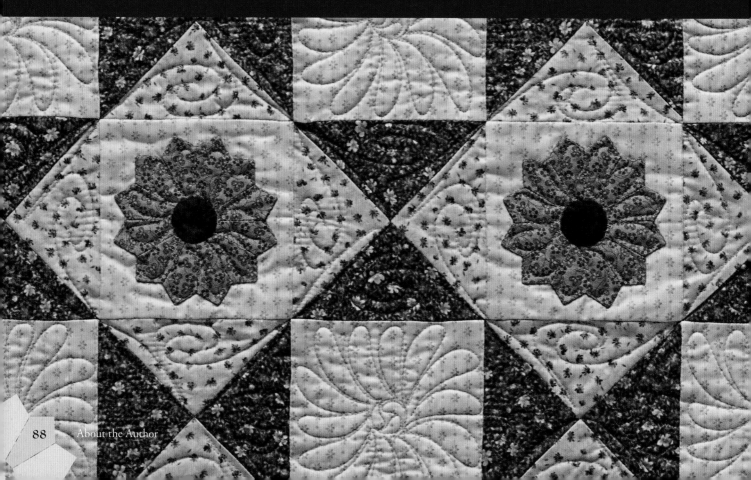